Product Rendering
with Markers

Product Rendering with Markers

Using Markers for Sketching and Rendering

Mark W. Arends

VNR VAN NOSTRAND REINHOLD COMPANY
New York

Copyright © 1985 by Van Nostrand Reinhold Company Inc.
Library of Congress Catalog Card Number 84-25677
ISBN 0-442-20952-5

Printed in the United States of America
Designed by Loudan Enterprises

Published by Van Nostrand Reinhold Company Inc.
115 Fifth Avenue
New York, New York 10003

Van Nostrand Reinhold Company Limited
Molly Millars Lane
Wokingham, Berkshire RG11 2PY, England

Van Nostrand Reinhold
480 La Trobe Street
Melbourne, Victoria 3000, Australia

Macmillan of Canada
Division of Canada Publishing Corporation
164 Commander Boulevard
Agincourt, Ontario M1S 3C7, Canada

16 15 14 13 12 11 10 9 8 7 6 5 4 3 2

Library of Congress Cataloging in Publication Data
Arends, Mark W., 1950–
    Product rendering with markers.

    Bibliography: p.
    Includes index.
    1. Dry marker drawing—Technique.   2. Visual
perception—Technique.   I. Title.
NC878.A7 1985 741.6   84-25677
ISBN 0-442-20952-5

For Linda, Elizabeth, and Christopher

Acknowledgments

I would like to acknowledge and thank the following people for their contributions to this book: Mark Bonnette, Ron Eckert, Dennis Huguley, David Sachs, Emily Pearl, George Tiston, Ed Zagorski.

I am also grateful for the contributions of the following organizations: Berol U.S.A., Chartpak, Eberhard Faber Co., Horizon Displays, Kitzing, Inc., Letraset U.S.A., Martin Instrument Co. (Mecanorma), Thomas A. Schutz Co., Walter Dorwin Teague Associates.

I am happy to acknowledge the many students I have had over the years who have wanted to learn, especially those who contributed their work for this book: Paul Degenkalb, Jim Haager, Brian Kolbus, Mark Kurth, George Simons, David Skinner.

Finally, a special thanks to L.J.S. for her criticism and support.

Contents

Preface

Nearly everyone is strongly attracted to the hundreds of beautiful colors and the slick packaging of markers. As with colored pencils, the potential for clean, bright, immediate color is very enticing; yet few people feel comfortable using markers for anything more than casual sketching. This is an unfortunate and unnecessary limitation. Markers can be used effectively to make convincing renderings of design concepts. Their versatility and convenience make them ideal tools for most visualizing tasks, particularly for graphic, interior, industrial, and architectural designers. Markers are easy to use. They require no preparation, dry instantly with little or no mess, need little cleanup, and are appropriate for many tasks.

In this book I hope to discuss concepts not covered in many marker books. By describing the visual dynamics of rendering and explaining the visual conventions used to describe products, I hope to provide designers with a better understanding of just what makes an effective rendering. I will also show how to apply these visual conventions to individual work to create impressive renderings and presentations. I hope these insights will encourage more designers to use markers and experience the pleasures of rendering.

Using this approach you may begin by simply enhancing line drawings with a minimal amount of marker. Then, with each successive rendering incorporating these visual conventions, you will build in more subtlety of marker use to produce full-color "realistic" renderings. Once these visual conventions are learned, you will be able to modify them and invent some of your own. They will provide you with all you need for most rendering situations.

The examples in this book come from three major areas of industrial design: product, automotive, and exhibit. Each of these areas has developed its own style, which can be seen in the examples, yet the thought that goes into each rendering is the same. There is also a strong carryover into interior and architectural rendering. The understanding of light and materials is the same, the particular conventions for indicating them differ.

In addition to being a strong communication device, rendering also forces the designer to think about the products he is illustrating. In order to render an object one must understand its form, how the various parts fit together, and what the surface details are. Rendering therefore serves as a design tool that helps us develop a concept and at the same time provides us with a visual representation of the idea to react to and evaluate. And all of this is accomplished without using a great deal of time or money. Thus, rendering and rendering techniques have become important steps in the design process.

Objectives of Rendering in Product Design

Mass production and the rate of technological change in our society have created the industrial design profession. The designer faces the difficult task of generating new forms that meet the needs of future users without ever having seen the product to be used. There is no model, experience, or test to evaluate the product (though the designer may have similar products or previous models to serve as guides). Therefore, the process of design must itself be the test and evaluation.

In the earlier craft tradition of design, a small number of products were produced and used. Modifications and changes may then have been made. A few more products were then produced and again changes made or new technologies incorporated. In this manner the product evolved. The impact of any problems with the product was small as there were not a great number of products or, by the time there were, the problems had been worked out through this evolution. However, as the pace of change increased, this process no longer worked.

The development of the household flatiron illustrates this. Below is outlined a brief evolution of the flatiron, listing features of each iron presented, followed by problems that promoted the production of the next iron. You can see how each successive iron attempted to solve the problems perceived in the preceding iron. However, you can also see that problems were only indicated by the failure of the preceding iron. Thus, for example, it was not until the third generation that any consideration of heat control was considered.

1. Solid Cast Iron: four or five irons were kept on the stove so there was always a hot one ready. Problems: you had to have too many irons. They were heavy and the handle was hot (figure 1–1).

1-1. Solid Cast Flatiron. This iron was cast as a single piece and kept hot by putting it on the stove. The handle got very hot; a number of irons were needed to ensure that an iron was always hot.

2. Slug Iron: a hollow cast iron accepted a hot iron slug to heat it. A wooden handle insulated the hand. Problems: you needed a number of slugs and tongs to move these slugs. Slugs were difficult to handle and were easily lost. The irons were still too heavy (figure 1–2).

3. Hot Coal Iron: this hollow iron which held hot coals was lighter than its predecessors and had no loose parts. Problems: dangerous spills could occur when loading. The iron was messy, still heavy, and had no heat controls (figure 1–3).

4. Gasoline Iron: this iron was much lighter. No messy, time-consuming loading was necessary, and there was a crude heat control. Problems: this iron was very dangerous. It was still heavy and awkward to use. Better heat insulation was needed for the user, and the handle design caused great fatigue (figure 1–4).

The evolution of the iron continued with the introduction of electricity and new materials such as stainless steel and plastics. It is interesting to note that the final solution to iron design may have come from fashion technology: synthetic fabrics have almost eliminated the need for ironing!

As technology changes, products will naturally change or evolve. However, many of the changes seen in the flatirons could have been incorporated into the first model had the craftsman been able to envision and evaluate the product before production.

1-3. Hot Coal Iron. Lightweight hot coals were put into this hollow iron to keep it hot.

1-2. Slug Iron. The original wooden handle is missing from this iron. A metal slug was heated and put into the iron to keep it hot.

1-4. Gasoline Iron. An effective, but dangerous gasoline burner was the heat source for this iron.

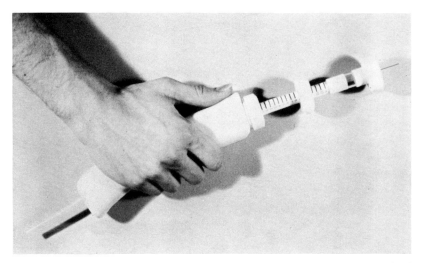

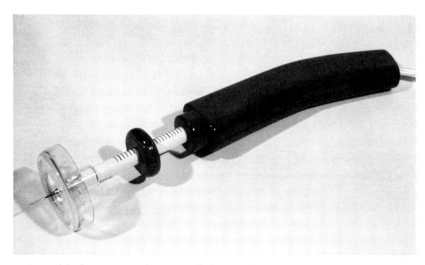

1-5. Mockup of a Cow Inoculator, David Skinner. This is a quick study model made of rigid foam, plastic tubing, and tape. It is used to evaluate a design concept quickly.

1-6. Model of a Cow Inoculator, David Skinner. This is a nonfunctioning model that the designer may use to evaluate or present a design concept.

As the designer replaced the craftsman and his task became specialized, he was separated from the marketplace and production and had to be able to design a product without ever making it, seeing it, or using it. When a product goes into production it must be appropriate to the technology and materials, have an attractive form, and be safe and durable. Speed in designing is also essential, as a product is appropriate for its time only. A particular design may be called "classic" and be in museum collections but changes in technology, cost of production, a better understanding of human factors, or changes in society make the piece more a collector's item than a response to current needs. This puts pressure on the designer and the design process. The consequences of a poorly designed product are great when multiplied by modern mass production and distribution. Economic failure, safety problems, or product failure can mean heavy losses for a company or injury to thousands of people. Therefore, one must be able to experience mentally the various possibilities for a product and communicate these possibilities to the many people involved in the product's development.

The effectiveness of drawing as a tool for thinking and the need for rapid development and communication of ideas have made rendering a basic tool for designers. (It is important to note that sketching and rendering are only some of the tools designers need. Good methodology, mathematical models, technical drawings, mockups, model studies, material tests, and prototypes are all tools a designer uses.)

The four steps in the design of a cow inoculator shown here (figures 1–5 to 1–8) illustrate how different forms of visualization are used by designers.

1. The mockup (figure 1–5) is a quick study model made of rigid foam, plastic tubing, and tape. It is used to evaluate a design concept quickly, particularly its form and size.
2. The surface model (figure 1–6) works both as an evaluation tool and a presentation aid.
3. Design orthographics (figure 1–7) communicate to a manufacturer or engineer the technical aspects of the design.
4. The rendering (figure 1–8) gives the viewer an idea of the appearance of the product as well as the materials. The side and top views show how the product will be held and used. Notice the rendering conventions used to indicate the transparent stop by the needle and the reflections in the handle. The dark area near the lower portion of the handle is a reflected horizon line; just below it is a line of reflected yellow light.

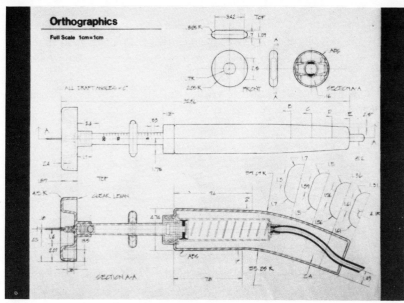

Orthographics

Full Scale 1cm=1cm

1-7. Design Orthographics of a Cow Inoculator, David Skinner. These drawings are used by the designer to communicate to a manufacturer or engineer the technical aspects of his design.

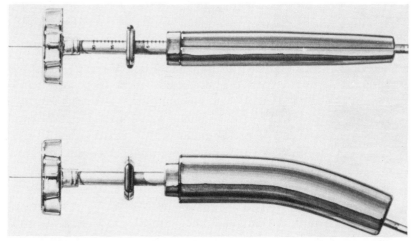

1-8. Rendering of a Cow Inoculator, David Skinner. Because this is an easy form to understand, an orthographic view may be used to render it. The rendering gives us an idea of the appearance of the product as well as the materials; the side and top views show us how the product will be held and used. Notice how the transparent stop near the needle and the reflections in the handle were rendered. The dark area near the lower portion of the handle is a reflected horizon line; just below it is a line of reflected yellow light.

Another design tool is the Interaction Matrix (figure 1-9). This is an organizational device used to cross-check elements to find critical problems important in the design of a product. To set up a matrix the designer lists all the parts of a product across the top and down one side of a grid. The type of interaction desired is then assigned to the chart; in figure 1-9 it is a physical attachment between parts of a popcorn popper. Each part is then compared to each other part. The value or strength of the interaction is assigned (usually represented with a graphic symbol), and put into the grid unit that corresponds to the two parts. For example, in figure 1-9, the switch (#2) has a strong physical connection to the fan (#6). This tells the designer that these two parts should be in the same housing, but there is flexibility in where they may

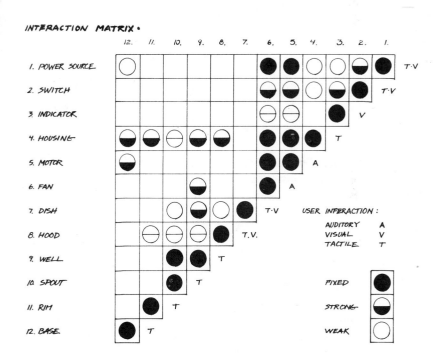

1-9. Interaction Matrix. A matrix is one method for finding critical problems important in the design of a product.

be placed relative to each other. A matrix such as this may be used to show a variety of types of interactions; e.g., parts to parts, parts to user, or parts to periods of time.

I would like to show very specifically how designers can produce effective, believable renderings to communicate their design concepts, the premise being that for a rendering to be believable it must satisfy certain visual conventions. Briefly, these conventions are: a sense of light and atmosphere about the object, and a consistent, comfortable rendering technique.

In order to understand and control the visual conventions, there are some basic guidelines one can follow as well as a number of "visual metaphors" that can be used like visual building blocks to construct a rendering. The guidelines are presented in the form of step-by-step procedures as well as suggestions or tips for more effective rendering. The visual metaphors are described and shown in examples. They consist of marker techniques that can be used to indicate a particular visual effect in a rendering—the marker strokes used to indicate the brushed aluminum surface of a control panel, for example. Once you learn these visual metaphors you will be able to modify them and invent some of your own. This system will provide you with all you need for most rendering situations, as well as help you develop a unique rendering style of your own.

The remainder of this chapter briefly discusses the content of and some techniques for thumbnail sketching, presentation sketches, full-color renderings, and illustrations. The drawing skills used in rendering are important at all these levels of design drawing. However, just as the visual quality and rendering involvement change at each level, the content and information contained in the drawings also change. A brief definition of these different types of drawing may be helpful before they are discussed individually.

A *sketch* is a quick freehand drawing, usually done in pen or pencil with few details. Sketches range from small doodle-type thumbnails to concept sketches that may be in color. A *presentation sketch* is a careful drawing, usually larger than a thumbnail, often with color and details. A *rendering* is a very carefully executed drawing showing what the product will look like. *Illustrations* are more elaborate than renderings and usually show more than just the product. They are often used in advertising.

In the overall design process, marker drawings develop as the product develops. Thumbnail sketches explore the problems; they are rough and vague. Since possibilities abound at this stage, thumbnails are plentiful. Presentation sketches are more complete. Ideas are coming together, and one wants to sketch possible products. Renderings show real possibilities. One can "see" the product and thus can show it to others, evaluate it, and make decisions. Illustrations sell the product. One wants people to identify with the product, so it is illustrated to build an image.

Thumbnails

At the onset of a design problem and throughout the process, simple sketches, doodles, and notes are generated as a means of thinking, generating ideas, understanding form, and exploring possibilities. These thumbnail sketches (figure 1–10) are a very personal, visual/mental communication process one has with oneself. The materials and tools used should feel comfortable and be convenient (an extension of the hand), and the style of drawing should be relaxed and unselfconscious.

The effectiveness of thumbnails as a thinking tool can be enhanced in several ways:

● Change the way in which you visualize. Draw in perspective, then orthographically (i.e., a plan or schematic view), then draw details (figure 1–11). Repeat this sequence as you work. Visualizing an object in different ways forces you to think about it in different ways. Perspective sketching deals with form and a whole product. Orthographic rendering helps with the specific layout and organization of a surface as well as the internal components. By developing details, a sense for finish and some of the manufacturing concerns are explored. Another advantage to working this way is that the product seems to pull together more quickly and more completely. Finally, you will find that your drawing skills develop faster, as you are not under constant pressure to perform (draw) well. You can fool around with details and not be worried if they look "funny." You will find that your skills will begin to transfer: the accuracy of orthographics will be seen in the perspectives, and the gesture and "life" of the details will begin to show up in the orthographics.

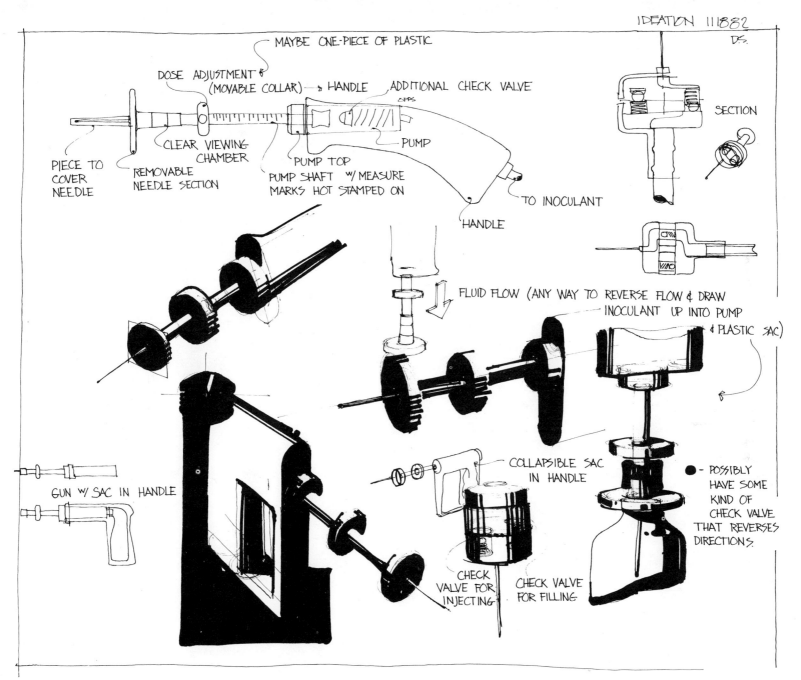

D.S.

MAYBE ONE-PIECE OF PLASTIC

DOSE ADJUSTMENT & (MOVABLE COLLAR)

HANDLE

ADDITIONAL CHECK VALVE

SECTION

CLEAR VIEWING CHAMBER

PUMP

PIECE TO COVER NEEDLE

REMOVABLE NEEDLE SECTION

PUMP TOP

PUMP SHAFT W/ MEASURE MARKS HOT STAMPED ON

TO INOCULANT

HANDLE

FLUID FLOW (ANY WAY TO REVERSE FLOW & DRAW INOCULANT UP INTO PUMP & PLASTIC SAC)

GUN W/ SAC IN HANDLE

COLLAPSIBLE SAC IN HANDLE

● - POSSIBLY HAVE SOME KIND OF CHECK VALVE THAT REVERSES DIRECTIONS.

CHECK VALVE FOR INJECTING

CHECK VALVE FOR FILLING

1-10. Thumbnail Sketches, David Skinner.

THUMBNAILS

15

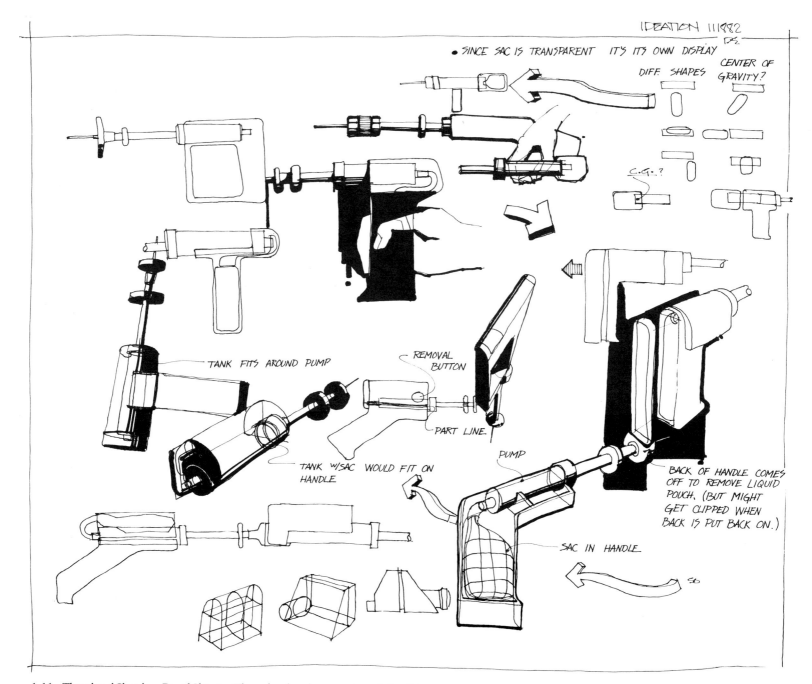

• SINCE SAC IS TRANSPARENT IT'S ITS OWN DISPLAY

DIFF. SHAPES

CENTER OF GRAVITY?

C.G.?

TANK FITS AROUND PUMP

REMOVAL BUTTON

PART LINE

TANK w/SAC WOULD FIT ON HANDLE

PUMP

BACK OF HANDLE COMES OFF TO REMOVE LIQUID POUCH. (BUT MIGHT GET CLIPPED WHEN BACK IS PUT BACK ON.)

SAC IN HANDLE

SO

1-11. Thumbnail Sketches, David Skinner. These sketches show a variety of visualizing techniques—some perspective sketches, some orthographics, and some detail work.

OBJECTIVES OF RENDERING IN PRODUCT DESIGN

• Do not always use "traditional" or standard materials. Tracing paper and felt-tip pens are commonly used for thumbnail sketching. You will find, however, that by changing materials you may experience a boost in creativity. The simplest way to do this is to change drawing tools when you are feeling "out of ideas." Fineline felt-tips leave a uniform dark line; broad tips put down a field of color; pencils can be light or dark and make gradations well (figures 1–12 to 1–15). Since the tools work differently, you will think differently while using them, and the drawings will look distinctive, thus providing you with additional information with which to continue designing.

The same can be said for papers (figures 1–16 to 1–19). In fact, I find yellow tracing paper too smooth for most sketching, though I enjoy its color and translucency. Many find the tooth (texture) and absorbency of newsprint very responsive to sketching. Drawing papers range from very smooth, hard surfaces that produce crisp lines to rough surfaces that give a textured, or even a broken line. Obviously, there are many possible combinations of tools and papers and, by having an assortment on hand, you can easily switch from one to another.

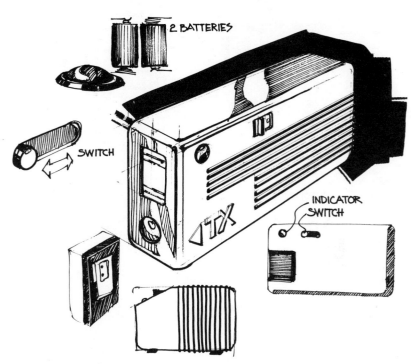

1-13. Quick Sketches. A medium-tip pen gives a bold line but discourages much loose sketching or shading.

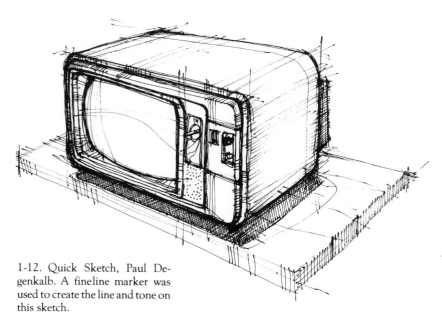

1-12. Quick Sketch, Paul Degenkalb. A fineline marker was used to create the line and tone on this sketch.

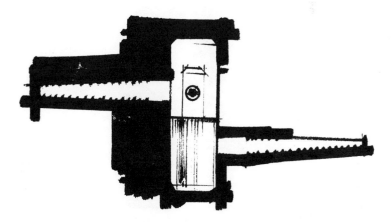

1-14. Broad marker strokes were used to "carve" out this hinge and show details such as screw threads on the shafts.

THUMBNAILS

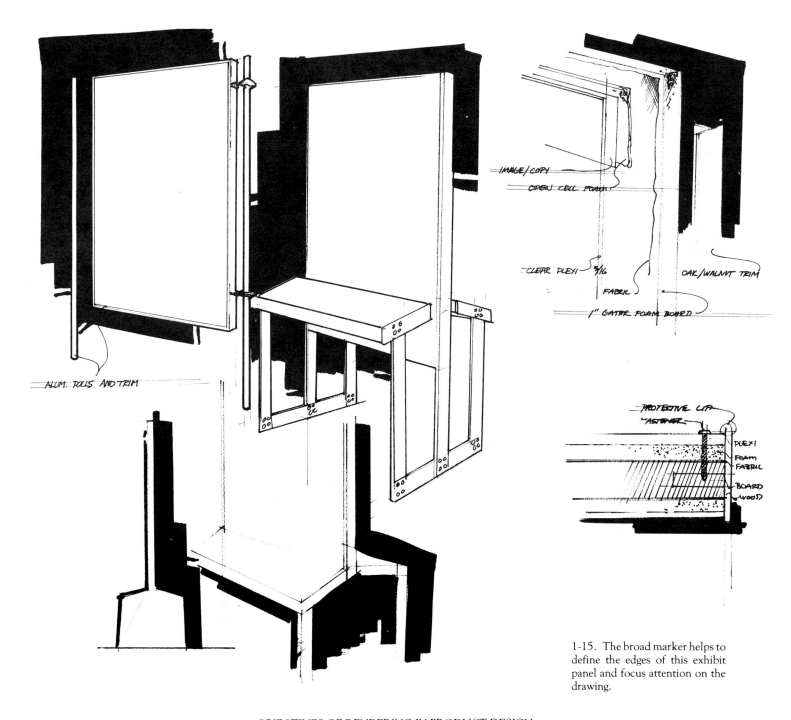

IMAGE/COPY

OPEN CELL FOAM

CLEAR PLEXI 3/16

FABRIC

1" GATER FOAM BOARD

OAK/WALNUT TRIM

ALUM. ROLLS AND TRIM

PROTECTIVE LIP

FASTENER

PLEXI

FOAM

FABRIC

BOARD

WOOD

1-15. The broad marker helps to define the edges of this exhibit panel and focus attention on the drawing.

OBJECTIVES OF RENDERING IN PRODUCT DESIGN

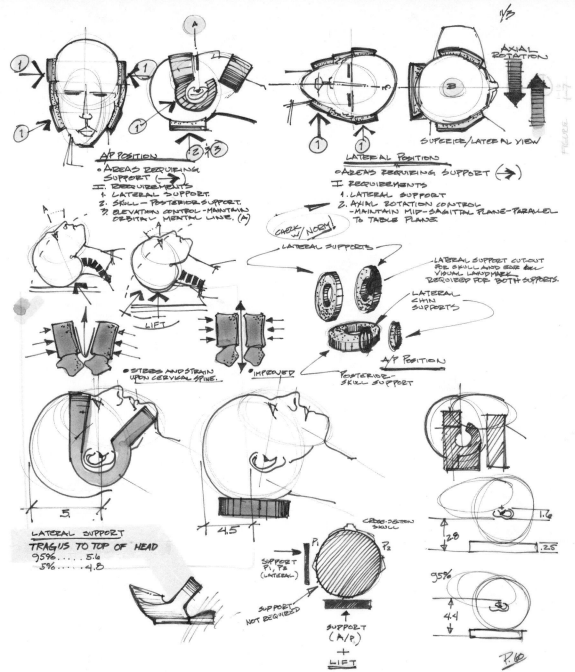

1-16. Sketching Done on Tracing Paper, Jim Haager. The lines are light and thin, and the color tends to be pale. This makes construction lines almost disappear once bold lines are added.

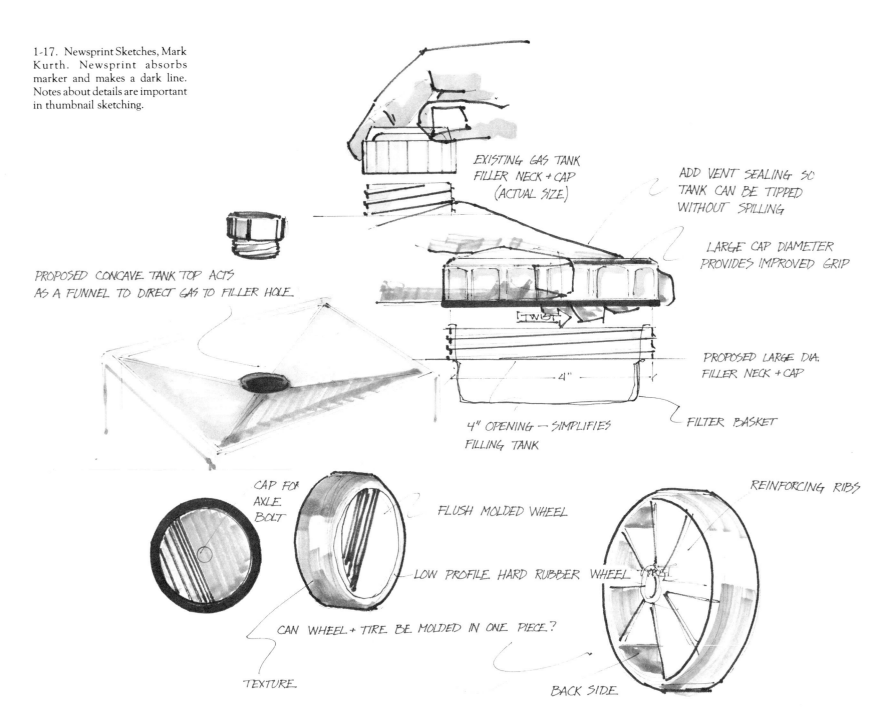

1-17. Newsprint Sketches, Mark Kurth. Newsprint absorbs marker and makes a dark line. Notes about details are important in thumbnail sketching.

EXISTING GAS TANK FILLER NECK + CAP (ACTUAL SIZE.)

ADD VENT SEALING SO TANK CAN BE TIPPED WITHOUT SPILLING

LARGE CAP DIAMETER PROVIDES IMPROVED GRIP

PROPOSED CONCAVE TANK TOP ACTS AS A FUNNEL TO DIRECT GAS TO FILLER HOLE

TWIST

PROPOSED LARGE DIA. FILLER NECK + CAP

4"

FILTER BASKET

4" OPENING — SIMPLIFIES FILLING TANK

CAP FOR AXLE BOLT

FLUSH MOLDED WHEEL

REINFORCING RIBS

LOW PROFILE HARD RUBBER WHEEL TIRE

CAN WHEEL + TIRE BE MOLDED IN ONE PIECE?

TEXTURE

BACK SIDE

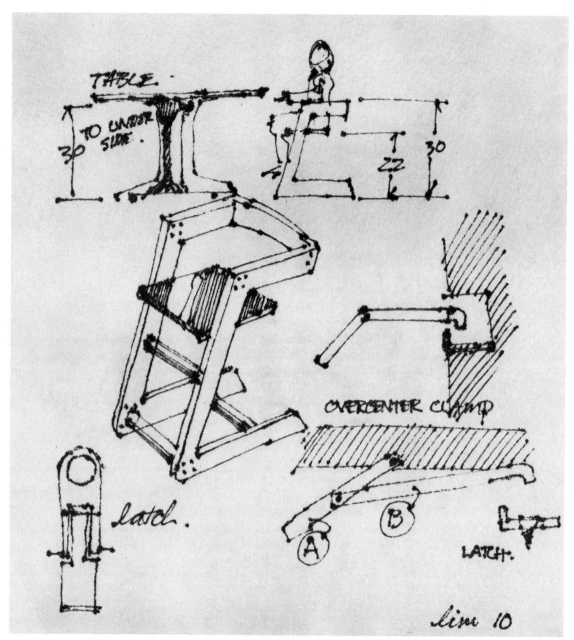

1-18. Thumbnail Sketches on a Napkin. Because of the absorbency of the paper, this felt-tip drawing is punctuated with dots wherever the pen stopped.

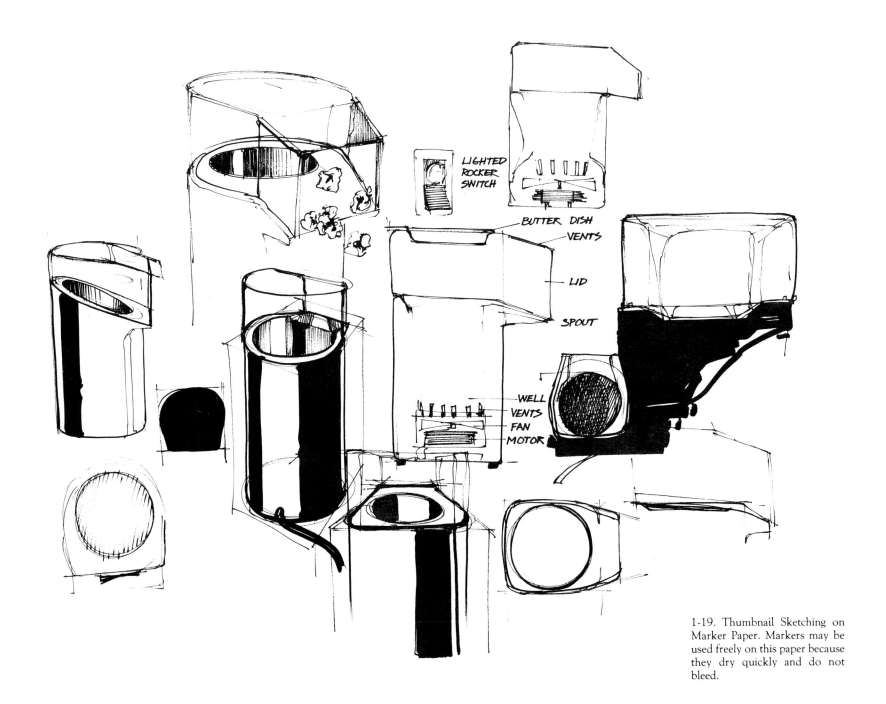

LIGHTED
ROCKER
SWITCH

BUTTER DISH

VENTS

LID

SPOUT

WELL
VENTS
FAN
MOTOR

1-19. Thumbnail Sketching on Marker Paper. Markers may be used freely on this paper because they dry quickly and do not bleed.

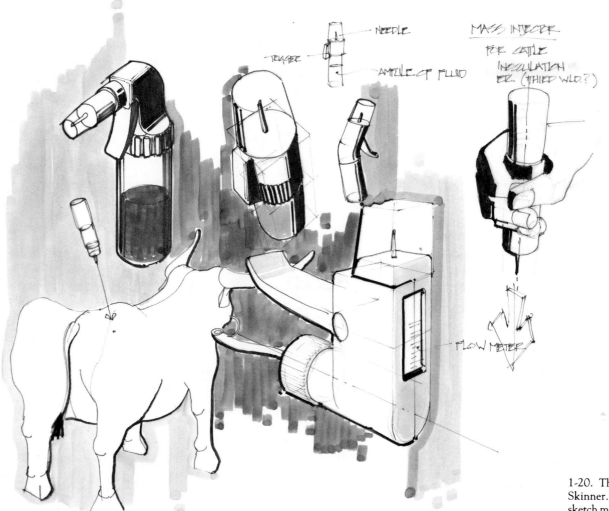

Within the sketch, the following handwritten labels appear:

NEEDLE
TRIGGER
AMPULE OF FLUID
MASS INJECTOR FOR CATTLE INOCULATION ER. (THIRD WLD.?)
FLOW METER

1-20. Thumbnail Sketch, David Skinner. Cartooning on your sketch may help you see the problem more clearly.

• Spend some time at ideation. Establishing a regular schedule and allowing enough time to become involved with the problem helps you become more productive and sharpens your thinking and sketching skills. Even when you have momentarily run out of ideas it is good to go back and casually render or detail an earlier sketch. This may seem like a waste of time, but it keeps you involved and may uncover a useful detail.

Another technique is to purge your mind of all ideas. Then draw all the new ideas you have, no matter how insignificant they may seem. You will find many new possibilities coming to you; they will continue to come all day if you do not censor them. The most common mistake is self-editing, saying to yourself, "I can't think of anything (good) to draw," or "That is too obvious or silly to draw." Drawing is like brainstorming in this regard: you must examine the inconsequential to find the significant. Good ideas are often created from seemingly insignificant or silly thoughts (figures 1–20 and 1–21).

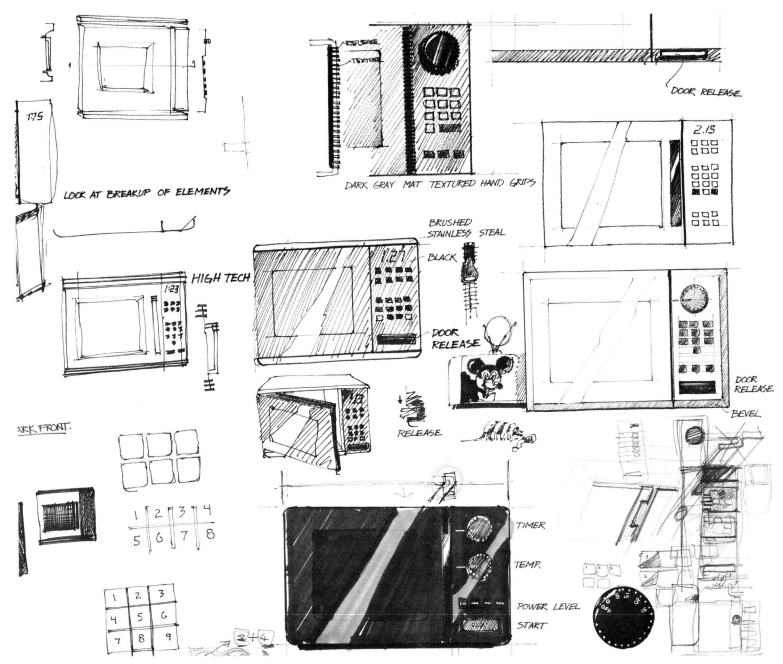

LOOK AT BREAKUP OF ELEMENTS

DOOR RELEASE

DARK GRAY MAT TEXTURED HAND GRIPS

HIGH TECH

BRUSHED STAINLESS STEAL

BLACK

DOOR RELEASE

RELEASE

DOOR RELEASE

BEVEL

TIMER

TEMP.

POWER LEVEL

START

1-21. Doodles on thumbnail sketches help relieve pressure and may provide an insight.

OBJECTIVES OF RENDERING IN PRODUCT DESIGN

• Think about form as it relates to product use when sketching. If a product is to fit into the hand it may need to be round, so draw it round. You can refine the form later. Explore form with your sketches without preconceived notions of what has been done before. Along with this do not concentrate on sketching. Think about the object. Allow the drawing to be ugly if it has to be; just get the ideas down and make notes about them (figures 1–22 to 1–24).

LOOK INTO ANGLES / · OF · WRIST
· TOOL   HEIGHT OF GRILL ETC.
FORMS

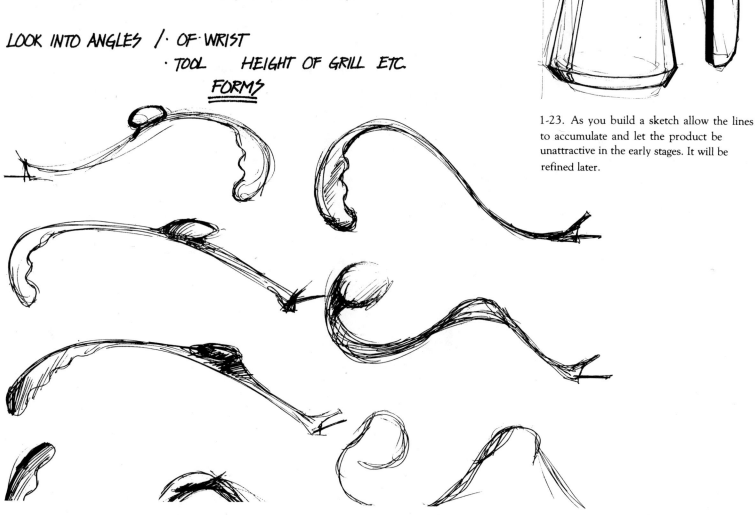

1-22. Freely sketching an organic form may be more effective than trying to construct it.

1-23. As you build a sketch allow the lines to accumulate and let the product be unattractive in the early stages. It will be refined later.

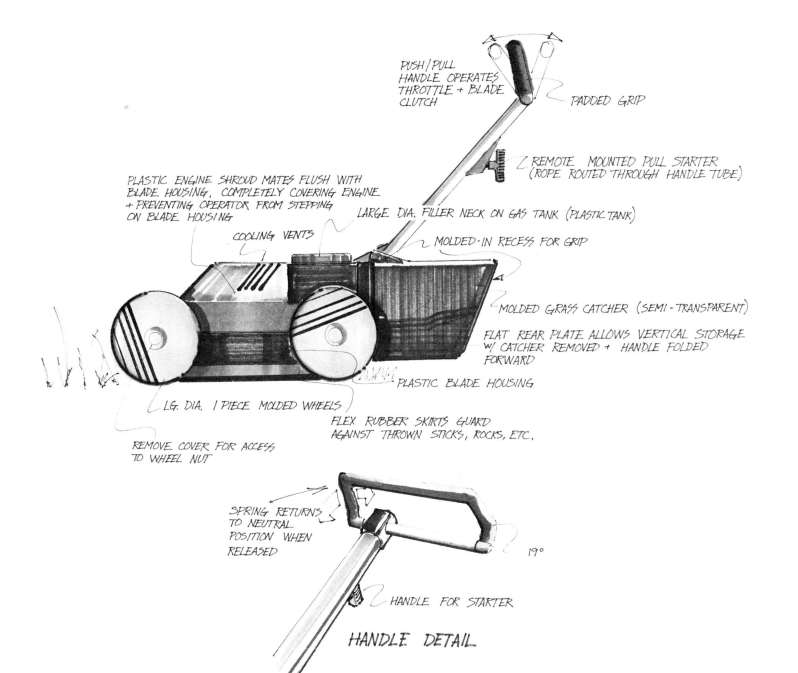

PUSH/PULL HANDLE OPERATES THROTTLE + BLADE CLUTCH

PADDED GRIP

REMOTE MOUNTED PULL STARTER (ROPE ROUTED THROUGH HANDLE TUBE)

PLASTIC ENGINE SHROUD MATES FLUSH WITH BLADE HOUSING, COMPLETELY COVERING ENGINE + PREVENTING OPERATOR FROM STEPPING ON BLADE HOUSING

LARGE DIA. FILLER NECK ON GAS TANK (PLASTIC TANK)

COOLING VENTS

MOLDED-IN RECESS FOR GRIP

MOLDED GRASS CATCHER (SEMI-TRANSPARENT)

FLAT REAR PLATE ALLOWS VERTICAL STORAGE W/ CATCHER REMOVED + HANDLE FOLDED FORWARD

PLASTIC BLADE HOUSING

LG. DIA. 1 PIECE MOLDED WHEELS

FLEX RUBBER SKIRTS GUARD AGAINST THROWN STICKS, ROCKS, ETC.

REMOVE COVER FOR ACCESS TO WHEEL NUT

SPRING RETURNS TO NEUTRAL POSITION WHEN RELEASED

19°

HANDLE FOR STARTER

HANDLE DETAIL

1-24. Lawn Mower Sketch, Mark Kurth. Making notes while you sketch helps to point out strengths and shortcomings of your ideas.

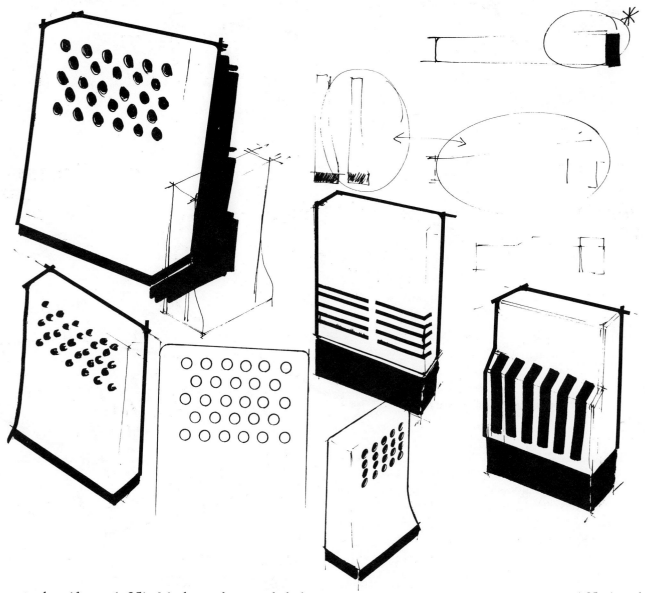

• Be sensitive to mistakes (figure 1–25). Misdrawn lines and dark smears can often suggest possibilities not yet considered. This also means that you should work quickly but review your sketches from time to time, even summarize them.

1-25. A misdrawn line may suggest a new form. Here a line suggests a slight sweep to the face of a product rather than a flat rectangle.

THUMBNAILS

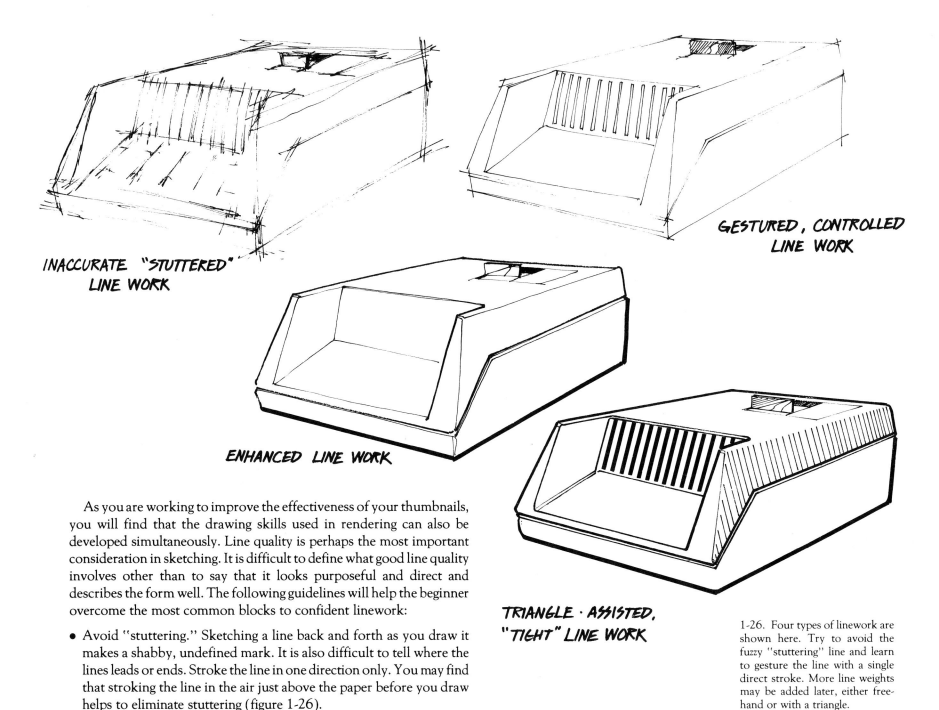

INACCURATE "STUTTERED" LINE WORK

GESTURED, CONTROLLED LINE WORK

ENHANCED LINE WORK

TRIANGLE · ASSISTED, "TIGHT" LINE WORK

As you are working to improve the effectiveness of your thumbnails, you will find that the drawing skills used in rendering can also be developed simultaneously. Line quality is perhaps the most important consideration in sketching. It is difficult to define what good line quality involves other than to say that it looks purposeful and direct and describes the form well. The following guidelines will help the beginner overcome the most common blocks to confident linework:

- Avoid "stuttering." Sketching a line back and forth as you draw it makes a shabby, undefined mark. It is also difficult to tell where the lines leads or ends. Stroke the line in one direction only. You may find that stroking the line in the air just above the paper before you draw helps to eliminate stuttering (figure 1-26).

1-26. Four types of linework are shown here. Try to avoid the fuzzy "stuttering" line and learn to gesture the line with a single direct stroke. More line weights may be added later, either freehand or with a triangle.

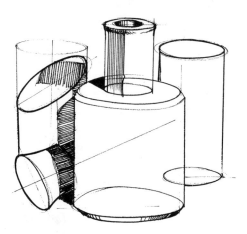

1-27. Various ellipses are shown here, each put down with a single gestural stroke.

- Gesture your lines, do not draw them. Conceive of the line as one stroke made with the hand and arm. The wrist should be almost locked. To make an ellipse, for example, first visualize it; then circle it in the air; then, with one quick gesture, put it down. Do not try to draw the ellipse slowly and carefully; it will never look right (figure 1–27).
- Control the direction of your lines (figure 1–28). Do not draw back and forth when drawing a series of lines. You will work as fast and with far better accuracy if you draw the lines in one direction only, a constant repetition of the same stroke. By putting the pen down at the starting point and looking to where you want it to go, the line will end there.

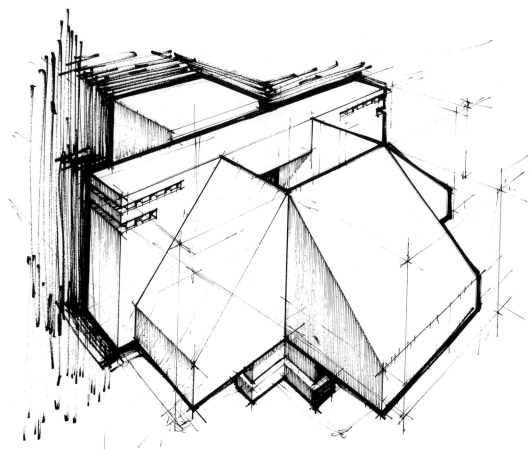

1-28. Line Sketch, Paul Degenkalb. A series of parallel lines effectively indicate shading. The linework is very controlled, being gestured all in the same direction with the same stroke repeated again and again.

THUMBNAILS

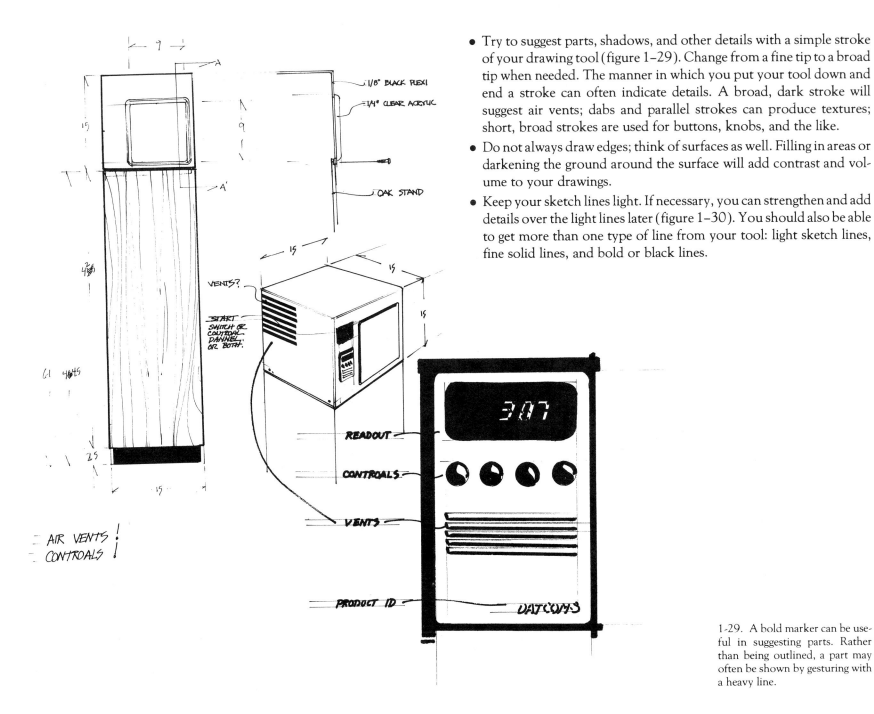

- Try to suggest parts, shadows, and other details with a simple stroke of your drawing tool (figure 1–29). Change from a fine tip to a broad tip when needed. The manner in which you put your tool down and end a stroke can often indicate details. A broad, dark stroke will suggest air vents; dabs and parallel strokes can produce textures; short, broad strokes are used for buttons, knobs, and the like.
- Do not always draw edges; think of surfaces as well. Filling in areas or darkening the ground around the surface will add contrast and volume to your drawings.
- Keep your sketch lines light. If necessary, you can strengthen and add details over the light lines later (figure 1–30). You should also be able to get more than one type of line from your tool: light sketch lines, fine solid lines, and bold or black lines.

1-29. A bold marker can be useful in suggesting parts. Rather than being outlined, a part may often be shown by gesturing with a heavy line.

As you can see from the examples, thumbnail sketching takes many forms and is very individual in style. Regardless of individual differences, thumbnails involve many levels of thinking and exploration. The depth of involvement will be reflected by the level of the drawings, from simple scribbles to elaborate sketches. When elaborate thumbnails are becoming more important and the designer needs to communicate to others, presentation sketches are made.

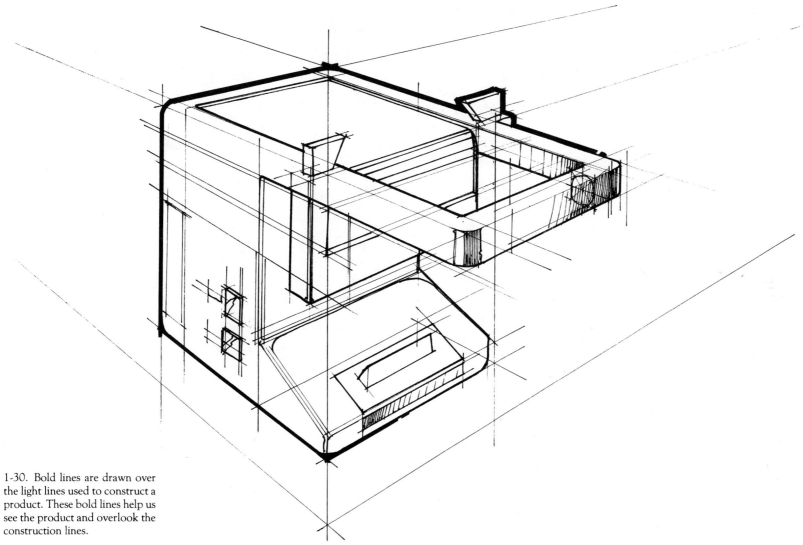

1-30. Bold lines are drawn over the light lines used to construct a product. These bold lines help us see the product and overlook the construction lines.

THUMBNAILS

Presentation Sketches

Once a designer is ready to communicate a concept she makes some presentation sketches. The concept is usually an idea that is given a temporary, unrefined form—just enough to make it look like a "real" product. This is often the point in a project where beginning designers will be asked to start generating half a dozen concept or presentation sketches for a given product idea (figures 1-31 to 1-33). One of the skills a designer must have is the ability to "see" and draw possible, appropriate forms for product ideas; in other words, to style them.

The power of presentation sketches is similar to that of a chapter summary in a text. They pull together many thoughts and feelings about a product and fit them into a concise whole. By doing this, relationships are made visible, details are coordinated, evaluations are made possible, and new directions are suggested. Once the basic concept has been accepted by the client, style becomes important, and you reach another, more subtle, level of designing. You can see that the act of drawing forces decisions about a product. In order to make a visual statement, be it a rendering, a sketch, or an illustration, you must understand what the lines you are putting down represent and how they will influence the use, manufacture, and sale of the product.

There are four basic forms of presentation sketches: perspective color sketches, orthographic renderings, line renderings, and diagrams.

Perspective Color Sketches

Perspective color sketches are used to pull ideas together into a whole. They are more elaborate than thumbnails, are drawn with color markers, and contain more details. Perspective color sketches are used for informal presentations to the design manager and/or the client. Often a number of them will be made to show possible variations of a concept. Perspective color sketches are also used to explore different color and detail possibilities for a particular product.

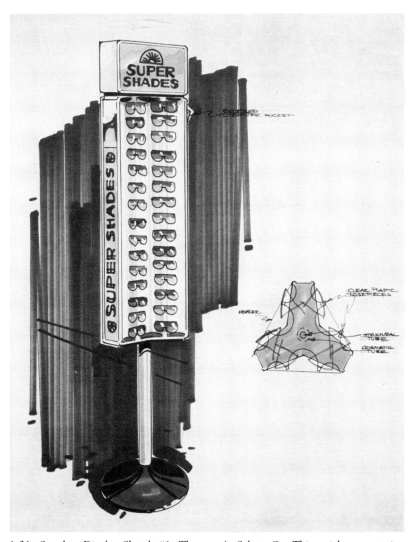

1-31. Sunglass Display Sketch #1, Thomas A. Schutz Co. This quick presentation sketch shows the basic form of the product along with notes and a top view to communicate the concept better. Markers are used in a very loose freestyle, and fine-line black linework is used extensively to delineate edges and details.

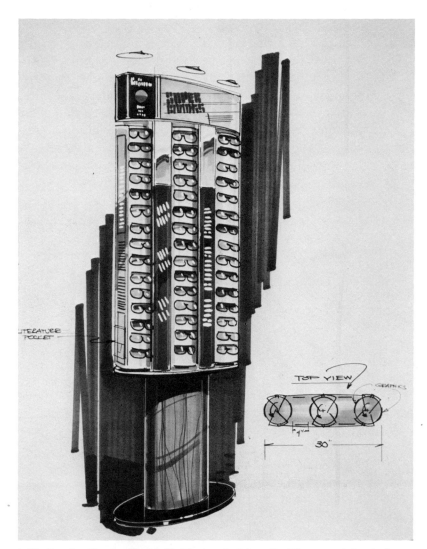

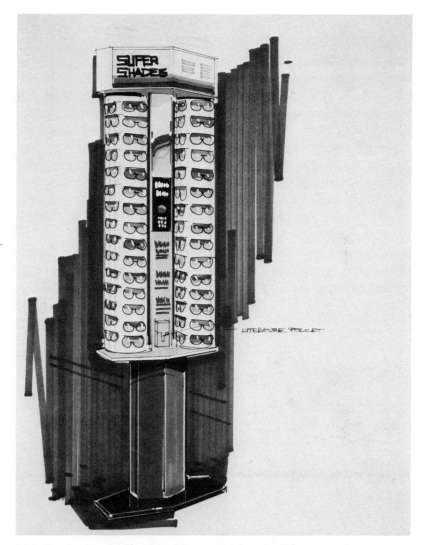

1-32. Sunglass Display Sketch #2, Thomas A. Schutz Co. This second sketch shows a different form for a sunglass display, but the concept of a freestanding unit on a post remains the same. Notice the fine brown lines used to show wood grain and the careful attention to graphics on the top of the display.

1-33. Sunglass Display Sketch #3, Thomas A. Schutz Co. Of interest in this variation is how vertical marker strokes are used to carry the post color into the base, making the base seem reflective. Note that each of these sketches is similar in style and layout, so that attention is focused on the design changes.

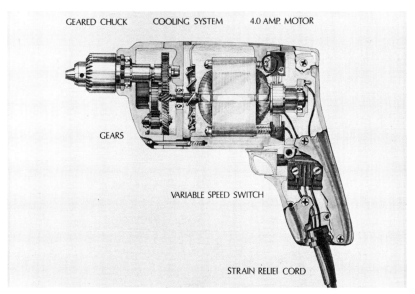

1-34. Orthographic Rendering of a Power Drill. Almost all of the components of this drill are cylindrical. Rendering it orthographically eliminates the complex problems of ellipses and perspective.

1-35. Detail of motorcycle rendering showing how markers were used to create the reflections on the gas tank and turn lights.

Orthographic Renderings

An orthographic rendering is a flat elevation drawing of a product (figure 1-34). Since there is no perspective used to show form, orthographics work best for flat objects, those with very little surface variation (e.g., control panels) or standard objects like cylinders. (See C1 in the color section and figure 1-35.) A simple orthographic layout of the object is made and then rendered to imply form and bring out details. This technique relies heavily on shadows and highlights for the rendering to read as three-dimensional. It is also a favorite technique among architects (figure 1-36) in the form of elevation renderings.

1-36. Architectural drawings are often done as orthographic views, relying on shadows and line weights to give a sense of dimension.

1-37. This line rendering attempts to show the transparency of the glass jar as well as the highlights and reflections on the product.

Line Renderings

Line renderings are quick, simple, perspective diagrams. They can be used for presentations or to "tighten up" a concept. Often you will have a number of good-quality thumbnails and will quickly make a perspective line rendering for presentation. The drawings are first sketched out, then tightened up with a triangle; exaggerated linework is then applied. Often one or more surfaces will be toned with marker or adhesive colored films (such as Zipatone). Line renderings usually offer only basic information about a product, vaguely indicating materials and surface texture. Details like controls, readouts, and vents are only generally indicated. However, the form and configuration of parts is clearly shown. A line rendering is to a full-color rendering what a foam-board mockup is to a finished model.

1-38. Line Rendering, Paul Degenkalb. An architectural line rendering is also concerned with light and shadow to show volumes.

Diagrams

Diagrams are often used in presentations to support a rendering or other visuals. The most common diagram is a mechanical drawing or schematic indicating how a part works or how it is assembled (figure 1-39). Diagrams may be in perspective or orthographic view, in color or in the form of line renderings. Often a diagram will use color to identify parts (see C-2 in color section) rather than show true color. However, the shadows and highlights used in rendering add to the visual effect of the diagram. A diagram offers functional information about a product and is usually very specific. Therefore, it does not offer the same flexibility or allow for as much discussion of design possibilities as does a sketch.

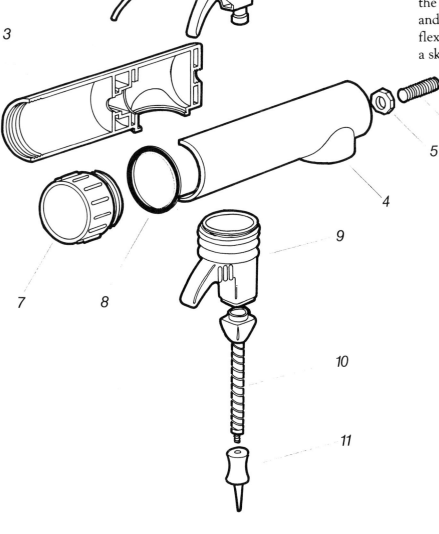

1 PUMP
2 PICK-UP TUBE
3 L. HOUSING
4 R. HOUSING
5 LOCK NUT
6 MOUNT STUD
7 FILLER CAP
8 'O' RING
9 PUMP HOUSING
10 FLEX TUBE
11 TIP

1-39. A diagram commonly used by designers is an exploded view. This shows both the parts and the basic assembly of parts. Line weights are often exaggerated in this type of diagram so that the confusion of overlapping parts is reduced.

Renderings

The primary purpose of a rendering is to communicate a design concept. It may be used for discussion within an office or as a formal presentation to a client or the public. Through the rendering a sense of form is given to the conceived product which, along with other information (more on this below), is the basis for an evaluation of the design. (See, for example, C3 in color section.) Because the rendering presentation consists of drawings, changes can be easily made if necessary. Renderings are quicker and less expensive to produce than models or prototypes and thus more flexible. Since there is usually only a minor amount of design development taking place when a rendering is being prepared, most of the effort is put into producing a convincing visual statement. However, the process of preparing a rendering may point up some design details that need to be resolved.

In addition to the form of the product, other information needs to be conveyed in the rendering. A sense of materials and surface is usually shown through texture and reflection of light. The purpose of the product is demonstrated by illustrating it in use or in a position ready for use. The scale of the product will be indicated to show how large it is and how it relates to its expected environment. The basic manufacturing processes of the product, as well as the imposed limitations on materials and forms, will be indicated by the placement of parting lines and the treatment of corners and edges. Finally, a rendering should show the graphic elements that will be on the product; e.g., operational symbols and company identification.

Two other considerations are important in a rendering. First, the rendering should focus on the important design elements. Backgrounds and unimportant details may be exciting in terms of composition and drawing, but they should be subordinate to the product. When these elements overpower the product, we are talking more of illustration and advertising than design rendering.

Second, the rendering is a sales tool. Its purpose is to communicate to and impress the client. For this reason you want the rendering to grab your attention, to "pop" (stand out), and keep the focus on the design.

Illustrations

The most complex type of design drawings are illustrations; these are very different from renderings. Illustrations are often used in advertising and promotion and are usually done after the product is in production. There is a strong emphasis on the "feel" of the drawing, and a number of dramatic techniques are employed to add greater impact to the composition.

The most common illustrating techniques are manipulated forms of rendering: selected rendering, in which one part of the illustration is carefully and fully rendered while the other parts are barely suggested by line; exaggerated or unusual perspective views that are used more for dramatic effect than to describe forms realistically; and the use of elaborate environments, showing the product in a desirable or theatrical setting to increase its appeal.

In addition to these techniques, an illustration often relies on a well-developed rendering style with a great deal of surface quality. The viewer becomes aware of the medium used to illustrate the product because it is so expressive, well-controlled, or bold.

These techniques of illustration may increase a product's appeal but reduce understanding of the product. They are also very time-consuming, making illustration an ineffective design tool.

Now that I have briefly introduced the basic levels of design drawing, it will be helpful to review some of the basic perspective and layout skills needed for rendering.

Elements of Perspective Drawing

Perspective drawing is a method for showing three-dimensional objects on a two-dimensional surface, giving the illusion of volume and space. It is an essential element in rendering, as it forms the basic linear structure for applying color. Drawings that are "out-of-perspective," or in which inappropriate perspective is used, are flawed from the start and will never seem "right," regardless of how well they are rendered.

It is important to have a good working knowledge of perspective for rendering and to be comfortable sketching in perspective. This will also help you to achieve a quick, easy look to your work that will give your renderings the freshness they need.

The two most common conventions for drawing in perspective are one-point and two-point perspective systems. They are named for the number of vanishing points used to construct a drawing. The basic difference between the two ways of drawing is in the way the object is viewed. In a one-point system, the viewer faces the front of an object and sees little or nothing of the sides. One-point perspective is primarily used for interiors in which the front wall is removed, allowing the viewer to see into the room. With two-point perspective, the viewer sees two or more sides of an object. Two-point perspective is thus more appropriate for drawing products.

There are two basic drawing approaches to perspective: mechanical set-up and freehand sketching. There are also numerous texts that do an excellent job of explaining the theory and mechanics of perspective (see Bibliography). I want to briefly review the steps involved in constructing a perspective sketch and the compositional elements of perspective that are important in rendering. Both of these will be illustrated by a triangle-assisted style of freehand sketching. Because mechanical perspective requires the careful use of triangles, T squares, vanishing points, and measuring systems, it is very time-consuming. Once the theory of perspective is understood (and with a little practice), freehand perspective sketching can be an effective and time-saving substitute for the mechanical method.

It may be helpful to go over some key principles of perspective before getting into actual sketching. For the purposes of this book we will be talking primarily about two-point perspective:

- Lines that move away from the viewer, called perspective lines, converge to a vanishing point.
- Vanishing points are located on the horizon line. There are usually

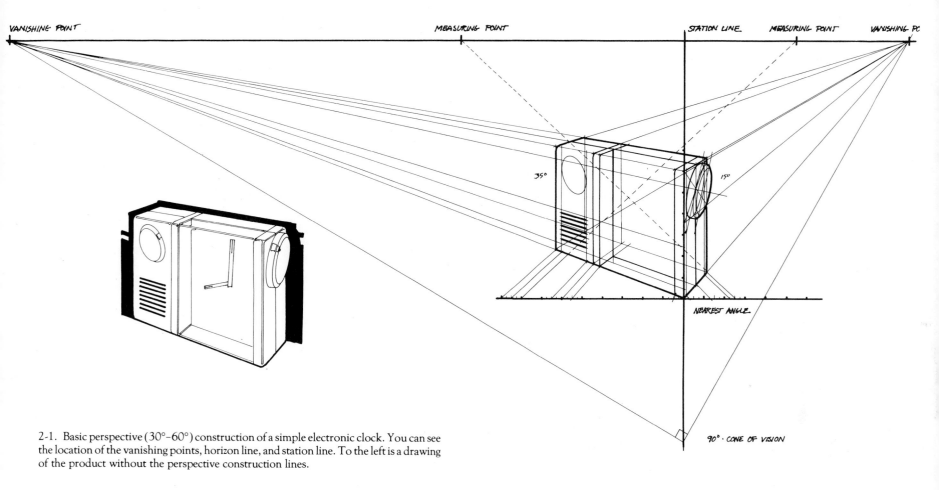

VANISHING POINT   MEASURING POINT   STATION LINE   MEASURING POINT   VANISHING PC

35°   15°

NEAREST ANGLE

90° · CONE OF VISION

2-1. Basic perspective (30°–60°) construction of a simple electronic clock. You can see the location of the vanishing points, horizon line, and station line. To the left is a drawing of the product without the perspective construction lines.

two vanishing points, one to the far left and one to the far right on the horizon line (figure 2-1).

- A station line runs perpendicular to the horizon line. This line indicates the viewer's line of sight; the object is drawn on this line or very close to it.
- The horizon line is a level horizontal line and is the same as eye level. For example, if you are looking down on a small object, the horizon line (eye level) is above the object (drawing).

- The nearest angle in your drawing (i.e., nearest the viewer) should be 90° or greater. This is called being inside the "cone of vision." If this angle is less than 90°, the drawing will look distorted.
- Vertical lines in a drawing are parallel and are perpendicular to the horizon line and the ground line.

If these rules are confusing, you should probably review a perspective drawing text before attempting to set up a rendering.

ELEMENTS OF PERSPECTIVE DRAWING

Perspective Construction

The use of perspective construction is probably the fastest and simplest method for setting up a rendering. The basic premise is to see the object as fitting into a series of basic geometric boxes. You begin to cut away at these boxes and add details until the form you want is revealed. The initial boxes may be drawn either mechanically or free-hand. The progressive refinement of the form will largely be done freehand, often using a triangle as a straightedge to keep the lines crisp. Utilizing perspective construction on the informal levels of thumbnail and concept sketching will sharpen your perspective judgment. Once proficiency is attained in freehand perspective construction, a good underlay for a rendering can be executed utilizing a T square and triangle. This will eliminate the time-consuming task of determining vanishing points and employing perspective layout systems.

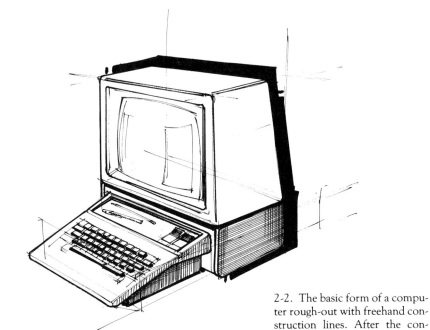

2-2. The basic form of a computer rough-out with freehand construction lines. After the construction is done, bold black lines are used to help separate the product form from all the linework.

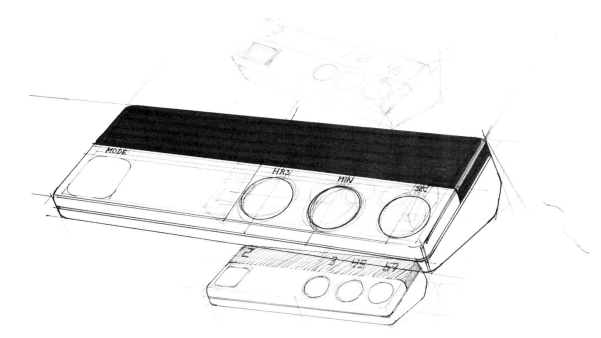

2-3. An electronic timer quickly roughed out using a triangle to sketch construction lines. With this method the construction lines are straight and crisp.

There are only a few basic steps for perspective construction that need to be learned:

1. Visualize the desired form in a box or combination of boxes. The box should have the outside dimensions of the object; parts can be cut away to get the exact form (figure 2-4).

2. Set up a basic perspective cube on which you can build more cubes and other volumes (figure 2-5). Then mentally cut away at them to reveal the form you want. For example, you might imagine a knife slicing off the corner of a cube to leave a beveled edge, or cutting out a recess for the controls. Select a convenient perspective system to establish this initial cube. (You may want to refer to a perspective handbook to refresh your memory about the various systems and their uses.) Be sure this cube is accurate, because the rest of the drawing is generated from this cube.

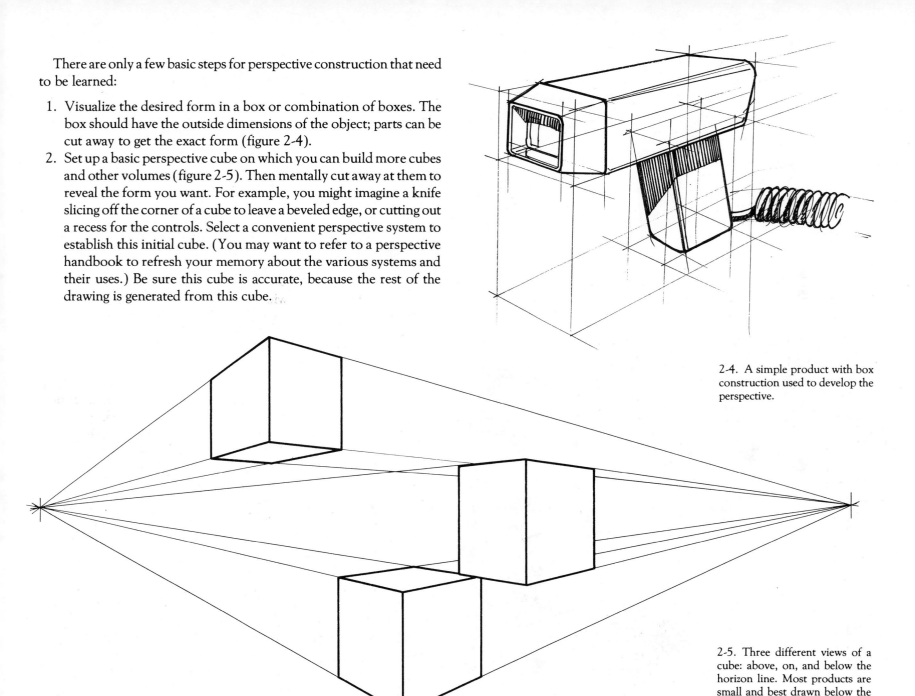

2-4. A simple product with box construction used to develop the perspective.

2-5. Three different views of a cube: above, on, and below the horizon line. Most products are small and best drawn below the horizon line.

PERSPECTIVE CONSTRUCTION

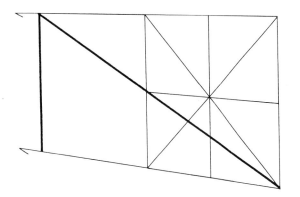
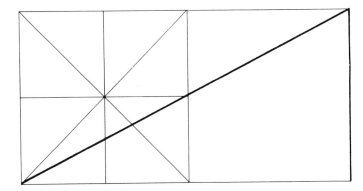

2-6. Multiplication of a square, using a diagonal (shown both orthographically and in perspective). This is the basic technique for multiplying a cube in perspective.

3. Multiplication and subdivision of the cube (box) is a simple geometric process. To understand the procedure it may be easier to work with squares and then put them in perspective on the box.

2-7. Photograph of the slide box that is the subject of the accompanying perspective construction.

To multiply a square, first find its center with diagonals. Then divide the sides in half with a horizontal line. Next, draw a diagonal from one corner through the center of the opposite side and continue it until it intersects the extension of the top edge. Draw a vertical at this point and you will have another square, the same size as the original (figure 2-6).

Imagine this square as the side of your perspective box and repeat the steps. Once you have the new square in perspective, fill it out to make a cube. The original box has now been doubled.

Subdividing a box involves essentially the same procedure. Taking a square again, find the center point and draw a horizontal and vertical through it. The square is now divided into quarters. Using one quarter as a new square, the same process will divide the surface even further. Again, use the square as a side of the perspective box and divide it. Fill out the rest of the perspective lines and you can cut off, or divide, the box in fractions of ½, ¼, ⅛, and so on.

A simple example (figures 2-7 to 2-16) would be to create a box 1 unit high, 1½ units long, and 1 unit deep with a clear top that would come down to the middle of the box. First draw a cube in perspective, then construct another cube next to it. This gives you a $1 \times 2 \times 1$ unit box. Now subdivide the back cube and you have the basic volume of your desired box ($1 \times 1½ \times 1$). To find the bottom edge of the transparent top, draw the diagonals in on one side. Their intersection is the midpoint of the side, thus the bottom edge of the lid. From here the details, such as rounded corners and soft edges, may be drawn in.

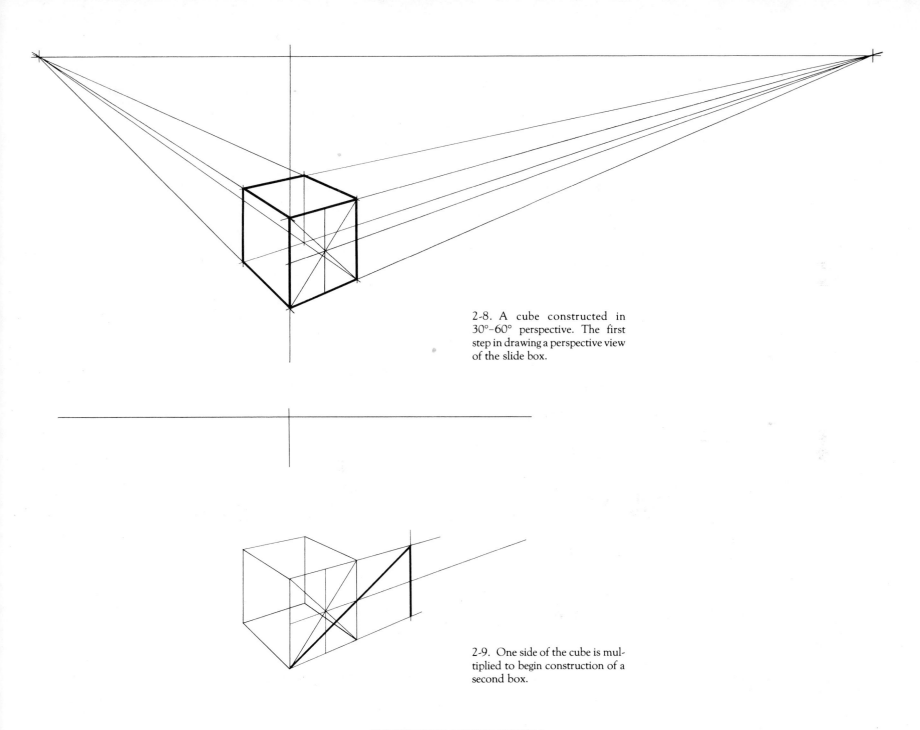

2-8. A cube constructed in 30°–60° perspective. The first step in drawing a perspective view of the slide box.

2-9. One side of the cube is multiplied to begin construction of a second box.

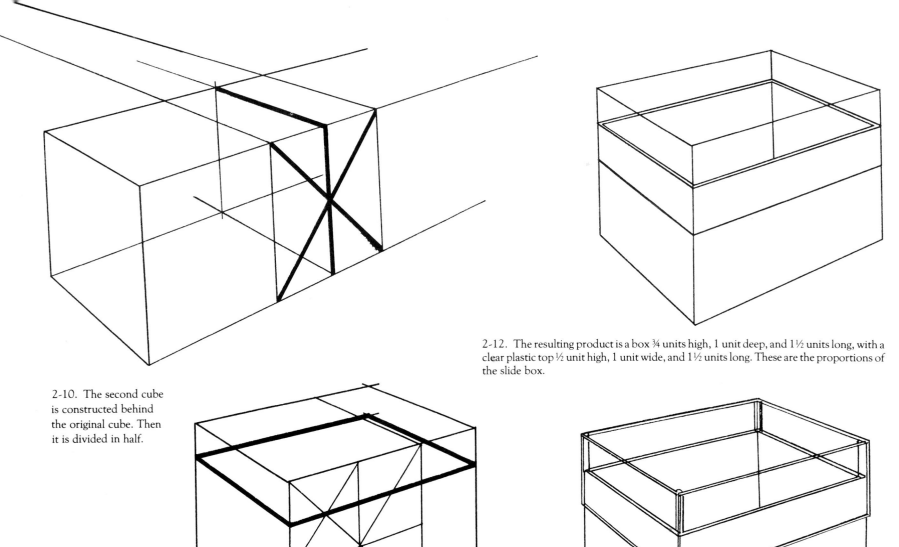

2-10. The second cube is constructed behind the original cube. Then it is divided in half.

2-11. The newly formed box is now 1 unit high, 1 unit wide, and 1½ units long. This box is now divided one-quarter of the way down from the top.

2-12. The resulting product is a box ¾ units high, 1 unit deep, and 1½ units long, with a clear plastic top ½ unit high, 1 unit wide, and 1½ units long. These are the proportions of the slide box.

2-13. Edge thicknesses are drawn in, and the rough box is finished.

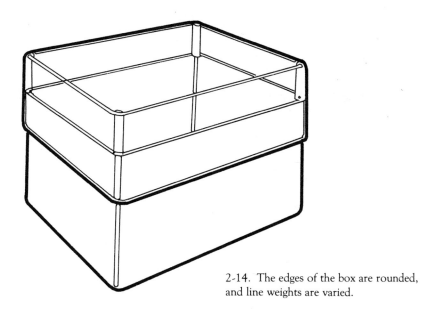

2-14. The edges of the box are rounded, and line weights are varied.

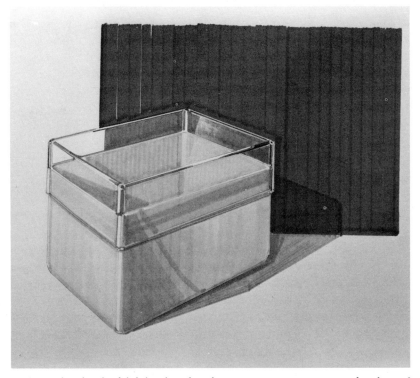

2-16. Marker sketch of slide box based on the perspective construction and analysis of highlights.

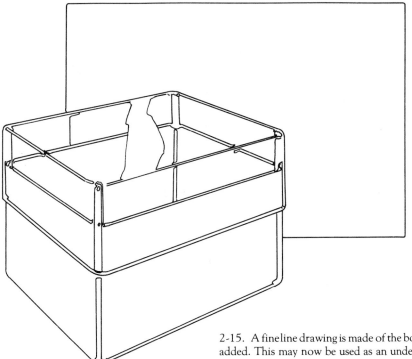

2-15. A fine line drawing is made of the box, and guidelines for rendering highlights are added. This may now be used as an underlay for a rendering of the slide box.

PERSPECTIVE CONSTRUCTION

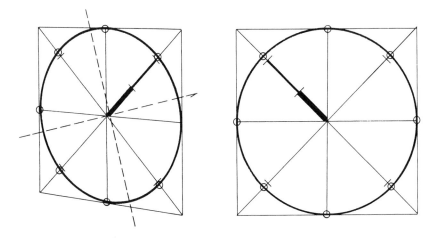

2-17. A circle in a square is tangent to the sides and hits the diagonals about two-thirds from the center. This information can be used to sketch an ellipse in perspective (shown to the left).

These examples should give you an idea of how to generate different forms. A general rule is to multiply the original box to get the large basic form, then to subdivide it to carve out details and locate parts.

One of the most difficult aspects of perspective drawing is making ellipses. Since an ellipse is a circle drawn in perspective, we can first examine a circle inscribed in a square. You will note that the circle is tangent to the square at the midpoint of each side and intersects the diagonals about two-thirds from the center (figure 2-17). When drawing a circle in perspective (an ellipse), construct a square, divide it into quarters, and draw an ellipse tangent to the midpoints and approximately two-thirds the distance from the center to the corner of the square along the diagonals.

A more elaborate method of constructing an ellipse is to subdivide a perspective square progressively and locate twelve reference points (figure 2-18). The first four points are the midline tangent points of the sides of the square; the other eight occur at the intersections of vertical and horizontal ¼-division lines and diagonals across their areas.

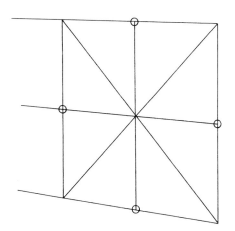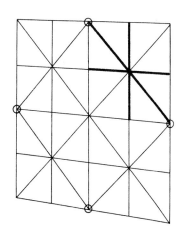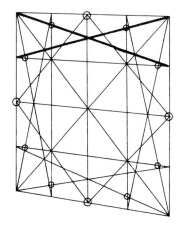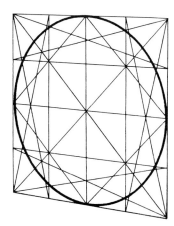

2-18. A more elaborate method of constructing an ellipse is to subdivide a perspective square progressively and locate twelve reference points. The first four are center tangent points on the square, the additional eight occur at the intersection of vertical and horizontal quarter division lines and diagonals across the area.

The task of putting in an ellipse is made a little easier and more accurate by using the major (long) and minor (short) axes of an ellipse to help construct it (figure 2-19). The minor axis of an ellipse moves in the direction of an imagined cylinder with the ellipse at one end. The major axis is always perpendicular to the minor axis. When adding the major and minor axes to an ellipse inscribed in a perspective square, you will note that the major axis is not the same as the diagonal (figure 2-20).

To draw cylindrical objects you will not need the square. Mark the outside edges of the form and draw in the major and minor axes. The minor axis will form a single line down the center of the cylinder. Major axes will be needed at any point at which the contour of the form changes. Finally, draw in ellipses at each major axis (figure 2-21). Remember that as an ellipse comes closer to eye level it thins out. So, the ellipses used to draw a bottle will be thinner at the top than at the bottom (figure 2-22).

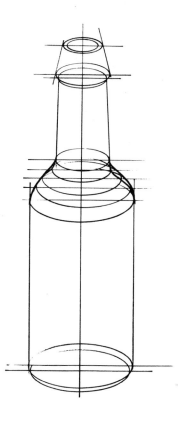

2-21. A cylindrical object can be constructed using a series of ellipses drawn along a vertical axis. Even more complicated cylindrical objects, such as a bottle stopper, are constructed in the same manner.

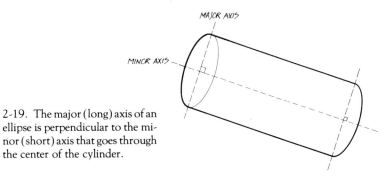

2-19. The major (long) axis of an ellipse is perpendicular to the minor (short) axis that goes through the center of the cylinder.

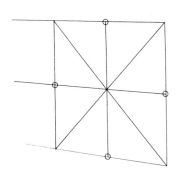

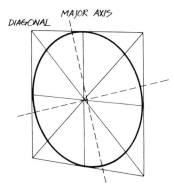

2-22. With construction lines removed, you will note the bottom of the bottle has a fatter ellipse than the top of the bottle, giving a stronger feeling of perspective.

2-20. The major axis of an ellipse is not the same as the diagonal of the square in which it is inscribed (but is often very close to it).

There are a few more conventions of ellipse construction that you should observe:

- The intersection of two cylinders forms a rough figure eight (figure 2-23).

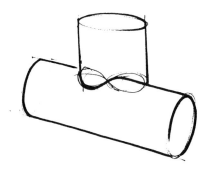

2-23. The intersection of two cylinders forms a rough figure eight. Using this knowledge, you can sketch a believable intersection without having to tediously plot it.

- To slice a cylinder or cone, draw ellipses at the high and low points of the slice. Draw a line from the high point through the center point between the two ellipses to the bottom of the ellipse. Using this line as a major axis, draw in an ellipse that is tangent to the side of the cylinder (figure 2-24).

- Remember that ellipses curve into the edges of a cylinder; there is no corner formed (figure 2-25). Creating corners is a very common mistake. To overcome it, lightly draw the entire ellipse and darken only the portion you need.

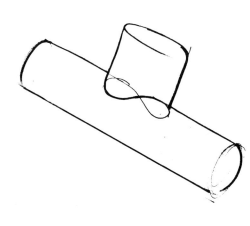

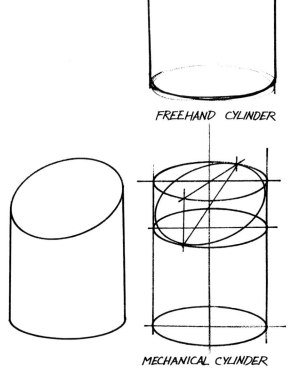

FREEHAND CYLINDER

MECHANICAL CYLINDER

CORRECT   INCORRECT - WRONG CORNER DETAIL

2-24. Shown here are both a freehand and a mechanical construction technique for sketching a cylinder with the top of the cylinders sliced off.

2-25. The bottom corners of a cylinder do not form sharp corners. They round into the sides.

ELEMENTS OF PERSPECTIVE DRAWING

Compositional Elements of Perspective

It is important when constructing your perspective drawing that it be well-organized and pleasing to the viewer as well as illustrative of the product. The various compositional elements can be divided into two categories:

1. Those elements that help determine the layout of the drawing and the organization of the page: choice of view, diminution, position/rotation, scale, convergence, and overlapping and auxiliary drawings.
2. Those elements that are important to the rendering of the object: focus, leading edge, shade and shadow, atmosphere, detail and pattern, and light source.

There follows a brief discussion of each of these compositional elements.

Layout and Organization
Choice of View

The selection of the proper view in which to draw an object depends upon what you are trying to show. The most you can show of a product in one drawing is three of its surfaces: two sides, and either the top or bottom (figure 2-26). All three may be shown equally, which gives a fair sense of the form; however, no one side will be seen very well. This equal view of three sides is rarely used in rendering. The designer will usually pick a view that shows one or two sides well and add additional drawings to show more if needed.

The most common of the three-surface views is called 45° perspective. This view shows the two adjacent sides equally and a small amount of the top. Another common view is called 30°-60° perspective. In this view one side is dominant while the other side and top are minimal.

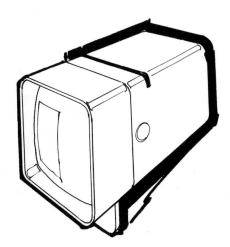

2-26. Slide Viewer. A three-surface view of a product gives the best description of its form. When all sides are shown equally, however, the product may look distorted as it does here.

Forty-five degree perspective is most often used for objects with two significant sides or for those whose form cannot be easily understood without maximum exposure. Such products include chairs, household accessories such as lamps, many toys, and mechanical parts (figures 2-27 and 2-28).

Often you will find that a product has one dominant side that either dictates the form (e.g., the side of a car) or contains the interactive elements (e.g., the face of a TV set). For these products a 30°–60° perspective is used so the primary surface is clearly shown, and the other two surfaces are used to give a sense of volume and form (figure 2-29).

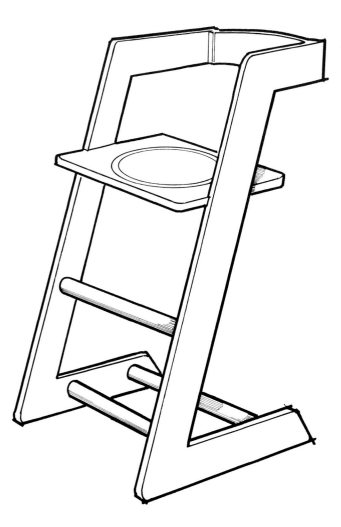

2-27. This 45° view of a child's high chair shows equal views of the front and the side. Both surfaces are important to understanding the form of the chair.

2-28. Rendering of a child's high chair done from a freehand triangle-assisted sketch construction.

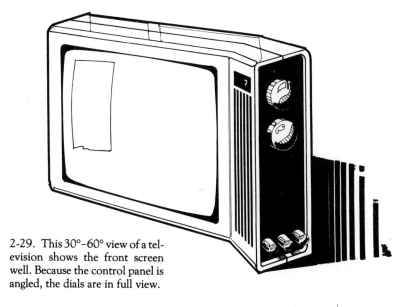

2-29. This 30°–60° view of a television shows the front screen well. Because the control panel is angled, the dials are in full view.

Another type of perspective is the straight-on view, also known as 90°, or one-point, perspective. Since this 90° perspective view only shows one side, a side, or section view will often be added to help understand the form (figure 2-30). A section view shows the open end of a product as though it were cut in half. Ninety-degree perspective is the fastest view to set up and render, but it works well only for very flat forms whose front surfaces have all the important information. It is also useful in communicating with people who are very familiar with form and design drawings. Generally, the understanding of form is greatly compromised in this view. For ease of setting up a 90° view, an orthographic drawing may be used. With careful rendering of highlights and shadow work, it will look in perspective (figure 2-31).

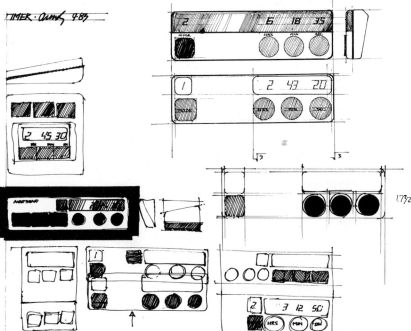

2-30. These sketches of an electric timer show how a side view can enhance the understanding of an orthographic drawing.

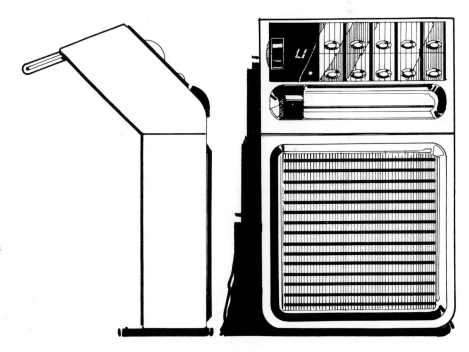

2-31. The side view of this orthographic of a portable C.B. receiver helps the viewer understand this form—one that is difficult to visualize when drawn orthographically. This product would be easier to understand if it were drawn in perspective.

Diminution

The next consideration is the natural view of the object to be rendered—how big it is, and how close the viewer is to it. A major element in this is diminution—the amount of convergence you see in the perspective lines as they go toward the vanishing points. In drawing, diminution is usually controlled by the distance between the vanishing points. The closer they are to each other, the greater the diminution. With diminution objects appear smaller as they are placed farther away from the viewer. With exaggerated diminution, objects get smaller very fast, and the perspective space appears shallow and stagelike (figure 2-32). With very gradual diminution, the perspective space appears stretched out and unnaturally deep. A general guideline for getting a natural looking space for your product is: the larger the object and the closer the viewer is to it, the greater the diminution.

Position/Rotation

Position/rotation refers to the natural setting of an object (usually when in use) relative to the viewer at a normal viewing angle. For example, a kitchen appliance is normally viewed on a countertop within

three feet of the viewer, whereas a television set is generally seen closer to eye level (as if the viewer were seated) and from further away. The position of an object will determine how much of each of its sides we see.

Scale

Scale (or proportion) is an important consideration when designing and rendering. In order to convey a sense of true scale, the size of a drawing should approximate the size of the actual product. Hopefully, a familiar part, such as a handle or switch, can be shown. If this is not possible, adding a figure, hand, or common object to the drawing will help the viewer to determine the scale of the product.

Convergence

Convergence refers to parallel lines that recede in space and appear to come together, or converge, at a vanishing point. The classic example of convergence is looking down a railroad track and seeing the rails appear to meet. This is very similar to diminution. In the railroad example, however, diminution would be used when referring to the trees along

2-32. Exaggerated diminution makes this car seem distorted and overly dramatic.

the railroad tracks that appear to get smaller as they get further away. The direction and degree of convergence tell us our position relative to the object, making the drawing more believable.

The following examples may help you to understand convergence. Hand-held objects and small objects that usually sit on counters or tables are generally seen from the front and top at close range. This dictates that they be drawn full-scale or larger-than-life, with a moderate amount of convergence. Large appliances and furniture-size objects are generally seen from further away, so they are usually drawn smaller than life. The convergence is slight, and the horizon line (eye level) is just above, or behind, the object. For very large objects—vehicles, architectural interiors, and the like—the viewer's relative position is very important. The closer the viewer is to the object, the greater the convergence and his awareness of size.

Convergence can also add to the drama of a drawing. Exaggerated convergence of perspective lines is very dramatic, even distorted at times. To neutralize a drawing and make it more of a diagram, reduce the convergence to the point where the drawing becomes an axonometric or oblique (parallel line) drawing (figure 2-33).

Overlapping and Auxiliary Drawings

The final elements that affect the perspective set-up and page layout are overlapping and auxiliary drawings. Overlapping helps us to read things in space and see them as three-dimensional. It is also a convenient technique for getting the rendered object to sit more comfortably on the page, as the overlap creates a transition from the object to the background and the page. Most commonly the objects overlap a background of some type. However, if there is more than one object to be rendered, by having the major object stand slightly in front of the other objects (overlap in the drawing), we get a real sense of the volumes of the objects, and they seem to be more closely tied together as a set (figures 2-34 and 2-35).

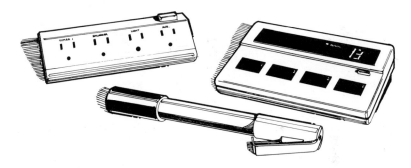

2-34. A group of products related to each other in design but not in composition.

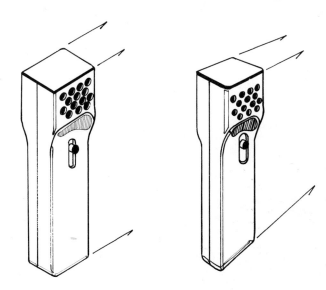

2-33. The parallel line drawing on the left appears awkward, while the perspective on the right shows lines converging toward a vanishing point; it appears more natural.

2-35. When objects are grouped together and overlap slightly, the composition is strengthened and the relationship between the objects appears to be stronger.

Auxiliary drawings can be an important part of a rendering as they offer additional information about the product. A perspective drawing of an electronic timer may have an auxiliary, orthographic drawing of the control panel to show layout and dial size (figures 2-36 and 2-37). An auxiliary drawing can also be partially overlapped by a perspective drawing and serve as a background. Another very common type of auxiliary drawing is one that shows the product in a natural-use setting. A car might be shown on the road, an appliance shown in the kitchen, and so forth. These drawings are usually in the same perspective as the object, but done in line, or a minimal "flat", rendered style (figure 2-38).

2-38. The background for this car rendering shows a flat, stylized suggestion of a tree line as a typical environment.

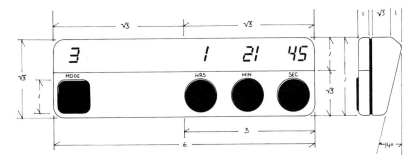

2-36. A dimensioned orthographic drawing that shows the relative proportions of the parts for the timer.

2-37. This electronic timer sketch was done in a minimal rendering style. The white paper serves as the top surface, with only the dark elements being rendered. This technique relies on linework to describe the form. An orthographic diagram was used as a background.

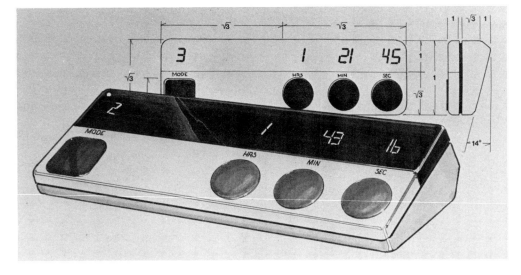

ELEMENTS OF PERSPECTIVE DRAWING

Rendering Guides

Once the perspective has been determined it can be set up either freehand or mechanically. This next group of perspective elements consists of those that affect the rendering of the object.

Focus

The focus of a rendering is the point where the greatest amount of attention is to be directed, both in executing the drawing and directing the viewer's attention. This usually requires developing details in this area. Use the greatest contrast, strongest colors, and do the most careful and elaborate rendering work in this area. Highlights, reflection, color, and shadows are very important in developing the focal area (figures 2-39 to 2-41).

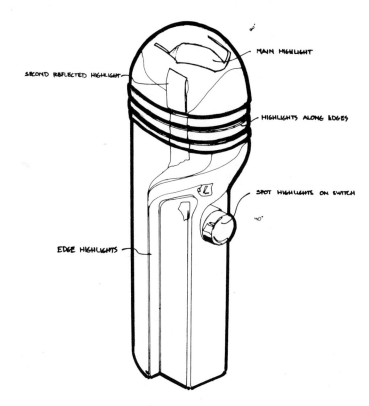

2-39. This line drawing shows the location of highlights on the product to serve as guides for rendering. This drawing was used as the underlay for a rendering.

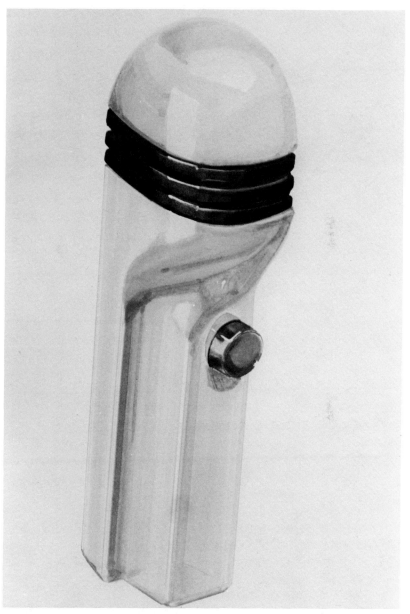

2-40. A rendering of a vertical hand-held stapler showing highlights on the leading edge.

By deciding on a focus for your rendering, you can quickly direct the viewer's eye to the most important part of the rendering. This saves a great deal of time since you do not have to render the remaining surface of the object thoroughly.

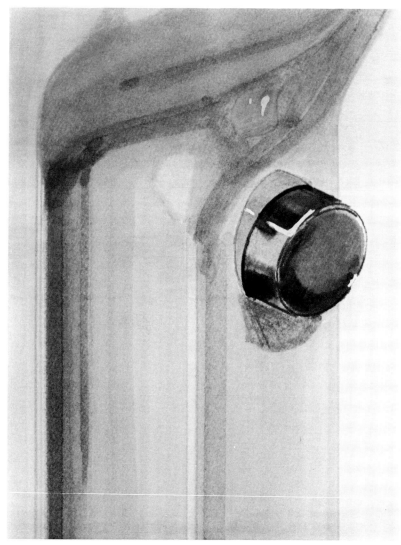

2-41. Detail of the stapler showing the loose application of marker.

Leading Edge

The leading edge is often a part of the focal area, but it does not have to be. It serves the primary purpose of pulling the rendering out of the page, causing it to pop forward and make the object seem three-dimensional. In the perspective layout the leading edge is the vertical corner in the center front of the drawing. The leading edge is usually defined by a strong highlight and high contrast between the surfaces that define it. It is often outside the background area, and it is from this edge that we perceive the convergence of the perspective lines going back to the vanishing points.

Light Source, Shade, and Shadow

These three elements are very closely related. The choice of the light source determines where the shadows will fall. It also determines where the bright areas, or highlights, of the drawing will be. In planning your drawing, you will want to have strong highlights in the focus area and on the leading edge. You will also want shadows falling to the back of the product, helping to define and set off the object in the focus area.

The shade side of the product is the side receiving no direct light. This should be the least visible side where little detail work will be done. The darkness of this side will, by contrast, make the focal area seem light and bright.

A useful concept when planning the highlights, shade, and shadows of a rendering is *chiaroscuro*. This is a painting term that refers to the play of lights against darks. Chiaroscuro can be used to develop the strongest contrast in the focal area. In order to do this you may have to gradate a surface so that there is a play of light and dark at the edge where it meets another surface.

Atmosphere

Atmosphere can be created in a drawing to help the viewer see the concept as a "real" product. Much like aerial perspective in painting, the effects of distance, air, and light are created by using less intense colors and fewer details for the more "distant" elements, and stronger, warmer colors, higher contrasts, and more detailing for the "closer" elements. An additional element that helps establish atmosphere is the use of reflections on the product from the background or from the parts onto each other.

Detail and Pattern

As you can imagine, it would take too long and become very tedious to try to draw all of the small details or accurately delineate the various textures and patterns found on a product. Therefore, it is important to selectively plan how, and where, to do the detail work. As you move from the focal area, gradually eliminate detail and generalize, fade out, or disperse the pattern and texture. It is also important to learn to approximate these elements simply and directly with marker technique, pencils, and chalk.

Some people find the technical, mechanical aspects of perspective very logical and master them quickly. Others have great difficulty with them. Either way, it is important to feel comfortable working in perspective in order to render effectively. Coordinating the compositional and rendering elements of perspective may seem complicated as you read through this, but the aim is to simplify the rendering as much as possible, while providing the necessary information for the effective communication of your product concept. You may find it useful to list the elements of perspective drawing outlined above and keep them as a reference guide to make sure that you are controlling the drawing to its best advantage.

CHAPTER THREE

Concept Sketching

Before we get into the specifics of marker use it will be helpful to examine the role of sketching and some of its most common forms a little further. Sketching is the basis for rendering, both in the exploration of form and in the development of skills needed for applying the markers.

Perhaps the most difficult aspect of rendering is understanding the subject. Sketching will help you explore various ways to present the object and force you to consider the placement of small parts and the location of rendering details such as highlights and shadows. For convenience, we can group thumbnails and presentation sketches under the term of concept sketching.

Purpose of Concept Sketching

As we have said, a major part of the designer's job is to give physical form to verbal concepts and to incorporate into that form many different concerns. Some of these concerns are self-imposed, while others are imposed by the client. They include aesthetics, human factors, and production factors.

Many of the concerns the designer deals with imply certain forms themselves. For example, a product that must be economically manufactured will, by implication, require no complex molds to make the parts and no elaborate hand operations in assembly or finishing. If a product is to be safe there can be no sharp edges and no exposed moving parts that can pinch. For safe, efficient operation the control area must be well laid out, and there should be visual access to working parts while keeping them physically separated from the user. The product must have an appropriate form as well as having aesthetic value; for example, a chair must structurally support the body, but it is also a sculptural element in a room.

In order to accommodate these and other considerations, the designer must be able to explore many different possible forms at many different levels—the basic form, the mechanics that go into the product, details, parts, and color. This is too complicated and important a task to leave to an unassisted mental exercise. The designer must record his thoughts about a product and learn from them, developing and refining each aspect of the design as he goes. Drawing and sketching become a way for the designer to think about design, to explore design, to talk about design, and to record her work, simultaneously. The following section briefly outlines these tasks.

Communication with Yourself

A dynamic relationship exists between drawing and thinking, and there are a number of ways that the designer can take advantage of this relationship to enhance his creativity:

- The paper acts as a memory. By recording thoughts on paper, they become a ready reference and may be reviewed to refresh your memory or to point out omissions in your designing.
- Drawing something from your imagination forces you to confront details and constraints that are overlooked when just thinking about it. The disconnected "dreams" are forced into possible concepts. However, since drawing a product does not require it to actually work, you can record these "dream" solutions without having to solve every problem at once and thus progressively refine the concept.
- The quickness of sketching allows for the expression of frivolous ideas that can be helpful in relaxing or seeing a different aspect of the problem, without forgetting the initial concept.
- Sketching aids in building a solution by progressive refinement of a concept or by allowing a quick generation of many different, but similar, solutions.
- The actual marks on the paper may suggest further directions or possibilities. Lines used to shade a sketch may suggest a texture or form change not otherwise considered.

Communication with Others

The power of drawing is impressive when used in conjunction with a verbal presentation of ideas. Drawings give direction and context to words. Here are some simple guidelines to follow in selecting or making concept sketches for presentation:

- The level of drawing must be consistent with the level of ideas. Do not go into details when you are not sure of them. The function of a concept sketch is to communicate an idea without letting the viewer become preoccupied with such elements as color, graphics, and texture, unless that is the point of the presentation.
- The sketch should be uniform in surface or finish. Do not elaborate on one area and gloss over other areas unless you are trying to create a specific focal point. Try to develop the sketch uniformly, losing detail and color only in areas of relative unimportance.
- Suggest elements such as color, texture, and materials, but do not overdo it. Generalized surface elements are easier to "see through" than detailed ones (i.e., you convey a "feeling for" the surface without using too much time or detail or focusing too much attention on it). You want the viewer to see, understand, and accept the *concept*. The surface elements and often the specifics of the form are still to be negotiated and resolved. A concept sketch will be far more generalized than a rendering.
- Marker strokes should be suggestive of detail elements on the product and add to the clarity of the drawing. Do not add unnecessary lines. Each stroke should be descriptive of the product and not added as a decorative element. It takes a great deal of experience to draw efficiently, but being critical of the marks you put down will help you develop efficient rendering skills.
- Clarity of the page is important. Add explanatory notes and support sketches in a simple, direct manner. Do not clutter the page with more than you need or with fancy layouts. Compose the page and give the major drawing room to breathe.

Remember, it is not how formal the drawing is, but its level of competence that lets it communicate well. A good presentation sketch is better than an overworked rendering. It will be fresher, more alive, and get the attention of the viewer.

Concept Sketching to Record Your Work

Aside from the bookkeeping and legal (copyright) aspects, having a record of your work can be very important to your creativity as well. As you look back over your sketches, you may find new answers. You will see the progress of your thoughts, perhaps see new ways to go, discover blind spots, pick up on an idea that was dropped but which later developments make significant now, or make a connection from two seemingly unrelated thoughts. To facilitate recording and reviewing your work these simple guides are suggested:

1. Work out a comfortable, consistent format in terms of paper size, organizational elements, and background styles. By making drawing more routine, you will find it easier to get started. A consistent format also makes the viewing of ideas less distracting.

2. Sign and date your work. There are some practical, business reasons for doing this. A designer's signed and dated sketch can establish a date of origin when applying for a patent. A designer's work can also be checked for an evaluation or by another designer joining a project. Signing and dating also help in reviewing work. The date records the sequence of the work. Changes in direction can be seen as a result of new insights or gaps in working time. Your pages can also be kept in chronological order.

3. Coordinate or bind your sketches. If your drawings are organized and simply bound they store well, encourage and simplify review, and do not deteriorate quickly.

This brief discussion of the uses of concept sketching should help you plan more efficient working habits of your own. You may also wish to try some different techniques of sketching depending upon the design problem at hand.

Techniques of Sketching

Numerous sketching techniques will add to your rendering skills and to your thinking about a product. I have created four general categories to help discuss various techniques: line sketching, value sketching, color sketching, and form sketching.

Line Sketching

Line sketching is the most common and easiest form of sketching. While it is very efficient and helps your understanding of perspective, it must be nearly eliminated in rendering. In line sketching, a line is drawn to show the edges of a form, the boundaries of an area (color, for example), and as a shorthand for common elements (typography, highlights, and detail switches). In rendering, by contrast, the edges are not drawn in, but described by the visual change from one rendered surface to another.

Line sketching can be a very simple outline, a cartoon, or a refined study of light and form (figures 3-1 to 3-3). It can be a very expressive gesture or a mechanical diagram. The first requirement of a line drawing is that it describe the form. This is usually an outline-type drawing and may be all that is needed. However, to this you may add different line weights, light and dark surfaces, highlights, texture, and shadows. By enhancing a line drawing with these elements it can become a good presentation tool.

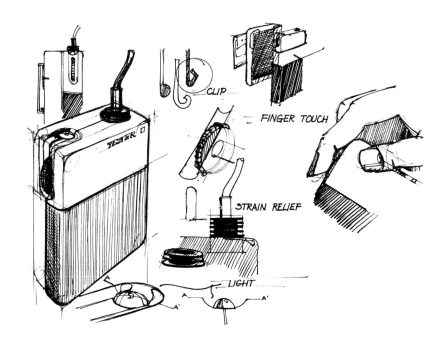

3-1. Very loose, freehand line sketches exploring different aspects of a product. Perspective form, orthographic layout, details, and interaction with the hand are all explored in a casual way.

Line Weights

A drawing done all in one line weight will look flat and, if done in fine line, weak and uninteresting. You should be able to draw a good bold line with your tool and, hopefully, a clean fine line as well (figure 3-4). A simple rule of thumb determines where to use light or heavy lines in a drawing: whenever both surfaces that make an edge are visible, the lines should be light. When only one surface is visible, the lines should be bold. Outlines are the boldest. Two additions to this rule are: background lines may be made into *vignettes* (unenclosed decorative line sketches that serve as a background to the main drawing), and front, or leading edges that are highlights may be drawn as two thin parallel lines. When lines are used to create a tone or shadow area, the line weight is usually light and the spacing varied to change value. However, shadow areas may be made with bolder lines than shade or tone surfaces.

3-3. This loose line sketch was done to analyze the location of highlights and shadows before making a marker sketch.

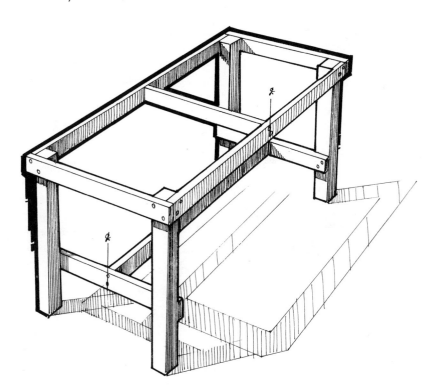

3-2. A triangle was used to get a very crisp mechanical drawing of this workbench base. Some shading and shadows were put in to help define the form.

3-4. Three line weights were used in this mechanical line drawing: a bold outline around the product, a medium line for interior edges, and a fine line to show highlights and reflections.

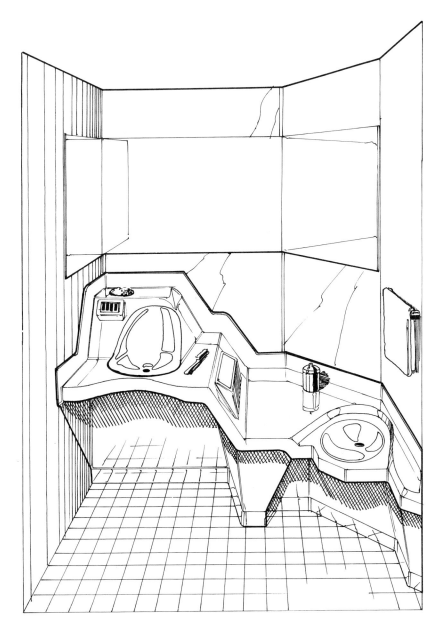

Light/Dark Surfaces and Highlights

Line is very effective in showing dark surfaces and highlights (figure 3-5). A series of parallel lines will darken and shade an area of a drawing. Highlights are usually done with a fine outline of the bright spot. Along an edge, the highlight is indicated by two fine, parallel lines drawn up to, but not touching, the corners. By putting a slight curve at the end of these lines, a radius is described at that corner. The space between the highlight lines indicates how round the edge is.

Texture and Shadows

To draw in texture the lines should be of regular character and put down in parallel, even strokes. The nature of the line will indicate the degree and nature of the texture (figure 3-6). There are standards for texture lines in architectural rendering that you may use (see *Architectural Graphic Standards* edited by C.G. Ramsey and H.R. Sleeper or *Rendering in Pen and Ink* by Robert Gill in Bibliography) or invent your own. To get shadows, remember that a shadow only exists as a lost or blocked light on a surface. Where a shadow falls, simply use a bolder line for the texture or a denser parallel line when there is no texture.

3-5. The very complex surface of this bathroom interior requires extensive linework to indicate highlights and shadows. This line drawing can be used as an underlay for a marker rendering.

3-6. By changing its weight and character, line can be used to indicate both texture and shadow.

Value Sketching

Value sketching is much different from line sketching, since it requires that you look for the pattern of light and dark to describe an object (figure 3-7). This is important to rendering because it is the contrast between light and dark surfaces that gives a rendering its volume and form. Linework, on the other hand, is primarily used to delineate small parts and details. When doing a value sketch do not look for the edges, but for the dark and light areas that create edges.

A common way to make a value sketch is to use the side of a piece of chalk or a soft, flat, carpenter's pencil and stroke broad areas of dark

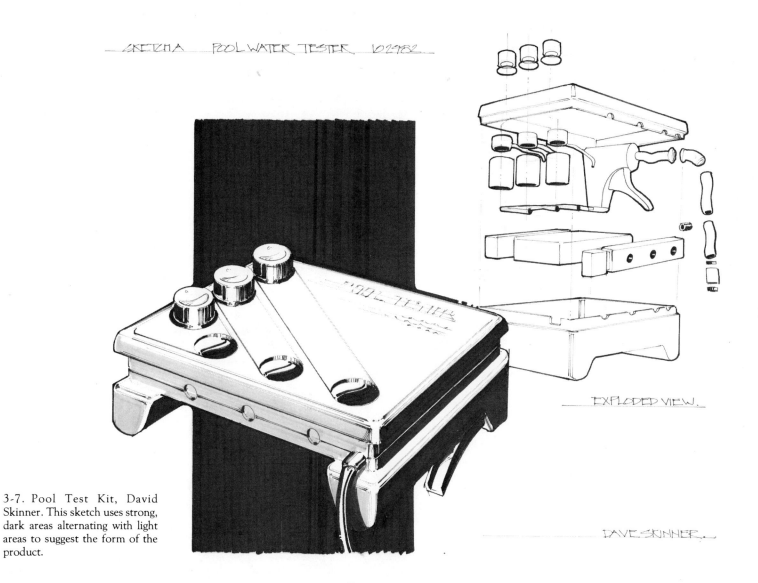

3-7. Pool Test Kit, David Skinner. This sketch uses strong, dark areas alternating with light areas to suggest the form of the product.

values to create a form. This obviously requires you to exaggerate values and to be more concerned with patterns and basic forms than with details.

Color Sketching

Color sketching is essentially a way of exploring the effects of color on a fairly finished form. Color is more complex than value, so we tend to simplify it when sketching. Because of this the drawings tend to become flat. Color studies are helpful to the designer. (See C4 in the color section.) Since the form is already understood, you can try to become sensitive to the subtleties of color.

For instance, you may find that primary colors can handle stronger contrasts and boldness both in their association with other colors and in the definition of the form itself. A bright red product may demand strong, even, playful details. However, a subtle curve or intricate detail on that red surface might be lost. With a more subdued color, such as a pale olive drab, the curve or detailing might become important. It is helpful, when sketching, to exaggerate the subtleties of color in order to find the right combination of colors and forms. You may also want to let the form, which was developed in line or value, respond and change with the changed effect once color is added. This will probably be a subtle change, but be sensitive to it. For example, in the design of a simple product such as a toaster, using a bright yellow for the housing might suggest a basic, casual form; if it were done in off-white, an elegant subtle form might come to mind.

Form Sketching

Form sketching allows a free play with the drawing tool to explore the form of an object. You may think of it as imagining the point of your pen moving over the surface of the form, rather than drawing edges or values (figure 3-8). It may be very gestural and free, or it may be very premeditated (e.g., drawing the outline of slices through the form, known as serial planes or sections). You will almost always have to come back to this type of drawing and pick out the lines you want, eventually translating it into a line or value drawing. I have found this technique very helpful for forms with very irregular cross sections, very organic forms, and forms that change along their length.

Sketching as a Basis for Rendering

One of the major problems of rendering is that one tends to get caught up in applying the markers and color, thus becoming focused on a very specific part of the rendering. This can cause many problems, including uneven contrasts, inconsistent light source, and poor detailing. You need an overview of the rendering and a guide or plan for doing it. The best way to achieve this is to use your sketches as studies. By doing this you accomplish three goals: first, you explore the problem and design of the product; second, you improve your drawing skills; and third, you eliminate the need for extensive value studies before doing the rendering.

For your concept sketches to work as studies for a rendering there are a number of things you want to make sure of as your ideas near a final form and are ready to be rendered for presentation of your concept(s):

1. Develop an understanding of the form. Draw the form from many points of view. Decide which viewpoint looks the best and try to eliminate any coincidence of edge or line that may make the perspective difficult to understand.

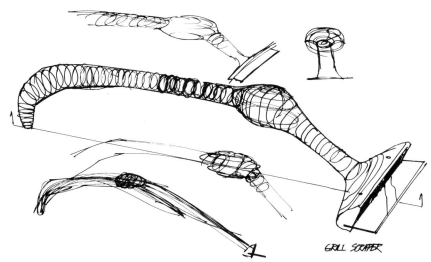

3-8. Sketching the form of a product may involve imagining your pencil moving over the surface of the product or, in this case, drawing the cross section of the product along its length.

2. Practice with the form so you know what happens to it. How does it interact with the ground (sit)? How does it curve around in back? What happens to the parts you cannot see (figure 3-9)?

3. Develop the form so that it is not too basic. Try to avoid any boxlike forms. Be sensitive to proportion, parting lines, edges, and curves. Be sure there is significant detail to make it believable. List all the details on a comparable product and see if you have accounted for them all, either by showing them in your drawing or by having designed them out (determined that they are not needed).

4. Explore the composition of the drawing. Are there simple line backgrounds or auxiliary drawings that will add to the understanding of the product? How can you give all the necessary information and have it well organized?

5. Look at reflections, textures, and shadows on your sketches. Determine the light source and contrast level of the drawing.

Sketching will help you explore and understand the product. You should become comfortable enough with the tools and techniques of sketching that you can make presentation sketches and be designing at the same time. From the presentation sketches you can then plan and execute your final renderings. The ability to understand an object as a three-dimensional form is very helpful to rendering successfully. It makes the understanding of light, gradation, and reflection necessary for rendering much easier and allows you to be less concerned with the application of the marker and therefore less liable to forget the form and function of the product.

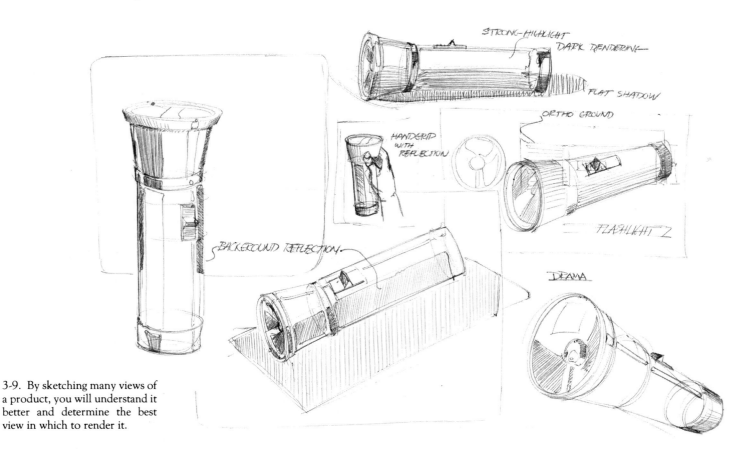

3-9. By sketching many views of a product, you will understand it better and determine the best view in which to render it.

SKETCHING AS A BASIS FOR RENDERING

Basic Marker Technique

Marker renderings will almost always be enhanced by other materials: Prismacolor pencils, pastels, a variety of papers, opaque white watercolor, and spray dyes. The majority of the work is done with markers, however. Below are listed some of the advantages of using markers as a primary rendering medium, followed by their shortcomings.

- Markers are very convenient and consistent. They are always ready for use. They require no preparation, and you can be sure of the color from use to use and when replacing a marker.

- Markers dry fast and produce very little mess. Because they dry very quickly, they smear very little and allow you to work at your own speed. There is no mixing, spilling, or cleanup to deal with.

- Markers come in a wide range of colors. They need no mixing, and with some careful selection and labeling you can have a good palette with relatively few markers.

- Markers can be easily adapted to different uses. In addition to rendering, markers are excellent for graphic layouts, enhancing notes, and labeling.

- Markers are inexpensive relative to other art materials and may be replaced one by one.

- Markers are fast. Because of the choice of a broad or fine tip, you can do linework and then quickly switch to a broad tip, covering very large areas.

- Replacement, storage, and transport of markers is very simple and easy.

- Markers are permanent. They will not rub off or be affected by sprays.

- Markers combine well with other media. Since markers dye the paper, they do not alter the quality of the paper in accepting other media such as chalk or paint.

The shortcomings of markers, like the advantages, depend upon the intended use. For rendering, we try to eliminate the following problems with technique and the use of other materials:

- Markers apply only flat color, and overlapping of strokes causes "stripes" in the rendering.
- You cannot "work the surface" with markers. If you apply too much marker, the paper becomes saturated and the color looks muddy. The marker needs to be applied once and left alone.
- As with all art media, using markers requires technique and continued experience.
- It is difficult to get gradations of color with markers. Since they dry very quickly, fast work is required to get a gradation from light to dark. This fast work can be very sloppy, and there is a tendency to put too much marker down, resulting in a dull or muddy color.
- Markers must be "broken in." At first they are too "juicy" and cause excessive bleeding and blobbing. Sketching with new markers on newsprint or another absorbent paper draws out this extra "juice." Markers also dry out, resulting in a light, streaky line.
- Markers perform differently on different papers. An individual marker will appear light or dark, bright or dull, will bleed or give a crisp line, dry quickly or slowly, all depending upon the paper being used. Select a few papers to use regularly if you want consistent results.
- Markers are permanent. With few exceptions you cannot erase markers, and when you can, there will be a stain left on the paper.

Because of the physical nature of markers, most marker renderings will have a similar look or finish. Considering variations for personal style and skills, marker renderings can still be identified by their clean, strong colors and the characteristic stroke of the broad tip. There is little subtlety of shading, and objects have a definite outline. To a great extent these qualities make markers good for product rendering. These qualities also make markers difficult tools for portraiture or more subtle drawing, such as landscapes. This chapter deals with the handling and application of markers to achieve the various visual effects desired in product rendering.

Marker Strokes

There are two basic ways to apply a marker: a gestured stroke or a drawn stroke. This is an important distinction, and it will greatly affect the drawing.

The gesture is a natural, "free" stroke. The complete line or mark is envisioned and an unselfconscious stroke produces the mark. It is not an entirely accurate stroke, but it imparts an emotional, alive quality to the drawing. The gesture is used very freely in thumbnails and sketching and, with more care, for laying down the first layer of marker in a rendering.

This technique must be practiced. The hand and arm must move through the whole stroke, while the mind envisions the line. Gestured strokes are very much like calligraphy in that you pull the marker. Here are some basic tips for gestured strokes:

- An ellipse is made all at once. Circle above the paper to "feel" the stroke, then touch the paper and gesture it in.
- Look to where you want the stroke to end. Your hand will move to that point.
- Do not be lazy. Move both the hand and the arm.
- Stroke in one direction only. Do not scribble-in an area.
- Develop a touch you can control, be it a heavy line or a light one. Feel the paper through the tip of the marker.

The drawn stroke differs from the gestured stroke in that it is a very mechanical, even stroke that is best suited for orthographic rendering, diagrams, and renderings in which flat color is desired. It is also good for "crisping up" or tightening a loose drawing and detailing and refining a rendering. When one makes a drawn line, one is very conscious of pulling or pushing the marker along. It tends to be a slower motion than a gesture, and the marker lays down an even, flat color.

Some general guidelines for a drawn stroke are as follows:

- Triangle-assisted drafting tools are often used to make a tight drawing with very careful edges. Using a triangle builds confidence for the novice because the strokes are clean.

- Try to box in details or leave them out; to draw everything mechanically is tedious.
- Forms become stiff as the markers go on flat. There is less chance for surface modulation or complex curves.
- The technique is very good for cleaning up loose drawings or putting down basic values.
- Because of the selfconscious nature of the stroke, the drawings take more time than do gestured drawings.

In general, a gestured stroke is good for sketching; as you slow it down and gain more control, it becomes the basis for rendering. The drawn stroke is a good technique for making a drawing crisper, for cleaning up rough spots, adding highlights, and applying colored pencil lines. Both have their use in rendering. The drawn stroke, being the easiest to master, will be the primary stroke for beginners. However, more and more of a rendering should be done with a gestured stroke once greater control is developed.

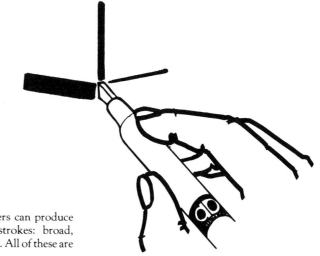

4-1. Most markers can produce three types of strokes: broad, medium, and fine. All of these are used in rendering.

Basic Manipulation of Markers

Markers are all basically alike in terms of how they put down color (dye). A variety of point sizes exists, ranging from very fine to broad, and each point size can produce a variety of different marks. The most common tip is a broad wedge-shaped tip, and most marker brands have a fine point. Experiment with different markers to become familiar with the kinds of strokes that can be made. Generally, each tip can make three strokes: a thin edgestroke, a medium endstroke, and a broad sidestroke (figure 4-1). In addition, a variety of dabs and dots can be made with varying pressure that will be useful for textures and materials (e.g., carpets) and details (e.g., lights and switches) (figure 4-2).

Blobbing, Overlapping, and Streaking
Once you become familiar with your markers you need to practice your strokes to develop a consistent, controlled hand. There is one frustrating problem here. New markers are very "juicy." When you draw a line it bleeds and leaves blobs wherever you stop. To reduce this

4-2. Exhibit Design, Material Expressions. The gesture stroke of markers is easily seen in the rendering style common to exhibit design. In this sketch a gestured stroke is used to show the carpet area, the reflection on the freestanding units, and the background.

effect the marker needs to dry out a bit. You can do this by leaving the cap off for a few hours. However, you risk drying out the tip and ruining the marker. A better method is to sketch with the markers on absorbent paper, such as newsprint, for a while.

There are a few guidelines for stroking with markers and creating textures. It will help to practice by filling in defined areas such as rectangles and circles. You will notice when you are stroking with your markers that as you put them down and pick them up they leave blobs on the paper. Also, whenever there is an overlap of strokes, the color builds up and is deeper, leaving streaks. These effects cannot be easily avoided, but when carefully handled they can add to the rendering. The first important guideline is always to stroke from edge to edge of a color area. Do not stop or start the markers in the middle or go back and forth across an area. You will get dark blobs if you do.

The buildup at the end of each stroke can work to your advantage as it increases the contrast for edge highlights and helps add a gradation of color to the area. As for the overlapping strokes, they often add to the manufactured, machine-made look of the product when drawn straight. When stroked in perspective, they help "read" the surface (i.e., help the viewer to perceive it) as going back from the picture plane (hence, in perspective).

Remember to keep the strokes going in the same direction, and if possible in the direction of the product. For example, if you want to enhance the vertical qualities of a door, stroke the markers vertically (figure 4-3). As you become more familiar with handling markers, you will find that the way you begin and end each stroke will help convey the nature of the material. Generally, the shinier the surface, the more the color and highlights seem to pool and flow into the edges. This effect can be created by pulling the marker down to the edge at the end of a stroke or stopping just short of the edge and letting it blob a bit.

Since the overlapping of marker strokes tends to build up color, you can adjust colors by overlapping different markers, working light to dark. The extent to which this can be done depends upon the paper you are using. As more marker dye is applied, the paper becomes saturated and will not absorb more color. If a marker is applied to a saturated paper, it will leave a shiny, discolored surface. Also, the white (or color) of the paper will be totally eliminated and you will lose the clear, bright color that markers usually have. The color will look dark, muddy, and

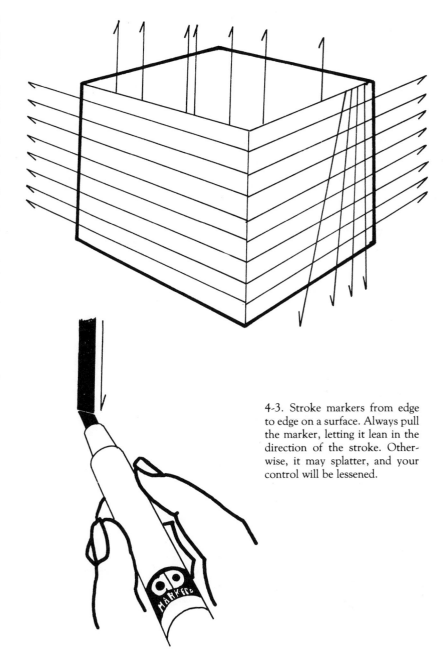

4-3. Stroke markers from edge to edge on a surface. Always pull the marker, letting it lean in the direction of the stroke. Otherwise, it may splatter, and your control will be lessened.

dull. I find it best to build up only three layers of marker and, on a color drawing, I try to keep from darkening a color with grays. Instead, I use a darker color or the complement of the color. For example, I might use red brown (cherry) over red to darken it, or a magenta over a dark red to darken it and "cool" the area. A green may be put down first and red over it to get a less intense, darker red.

If the streaking caused by overlapping marker strokes is annoying, there are two ways to eliminate it. Both methods have shortcomings that you may find more distracting than the streaking. The first technique is to use a nonabsorbent paper, such as vellum, and blend a light and dark marker. The light marker is applied over the surface. Then, working quickly before the marker color dries, the darker marker is applied in one area. Again, working quickly, apply the light marker and blend out the edges of the dark marker into the light one. There are disadvantages to this technique. It requires fast work that can often be sloppy, and if the paper is too hard (nonabsorbent) the marker color will pool and leave dark spots. Also, a light marker, when put over a darker one, may pick up the dark color into its nib, leaving a light streak.

The second method of avoiding marker streaks is to use an absorbent layout paper. This paper bleeds enough to enable the overlapping areas to bleed together and eliminate streaking. The obvious shortcoming of this technique is that the bleeding that occurs at the edges of the drawing requires some heavy linework to crisp up the edges. The rendering may look heavy and dull as a result.

Creating Textures

Another basic marker manipulation is used in creating texture. In sketching this can be very simple and direct—dabbing the marker to get a carpetlike look, or using short jabs for plant leaves. On a rendering, however, it is more difficult to make these texture strokes look right. They are still quick strokes, but patience and care are required to put them in the right places. When drawing a texture you will need at least three markers to show the lights, darks, and color changes. Before rendering texture, examine or analyze the surface carefully with an eye for the following:

- Determine how much light is falling on the surface. Locate the light and dark areas.

- Find the basic colors that make up the surface. Be aware that overlapping of markers will create mixed colors.

- Decide on the textured patterns as distinct from the printed design or color design. Choose marker strokes to simulate the desired patterns.

- Carefully plan out the area for marker application. Put down the light values first and work to the dark.

- Do not overlook the printed pattern. You will have to change to other color markers as the pattern changes.

Rendering Basic Volumes and Simple Objects

Through the following examples I want to show the basic conventions, or visual metaphors, for describing volumes, materials, highlights, and surfaces. The simplest way to render a form is to define a light source and show how different parts of that form are affected by the light. Normally, you will find there are three primary value surfaces and a shadow area.

Value Range

To render objects you will need to establish a range of values with your gray markers. There are two choices when choosing gray markers: warm grays and cool grays. The warm grays are slightly on the brown or tan side, and the cool grays are bluish in color (figure 4-4). Either set works fine, but they should not be mixed. Cool grays are good for white metals, such as aluminum, and appear to be truer than warm grays. Warm grays are good for interior and architectural work, since they work well with the earth tones found in building materials. With your markers make a gray scale (numbered one through ten) from white to black, with zero representing white and ten representing black. You will work from this gray scale to select values for rendering. The numbering system is important for planning drawings, as you will see.

There are three primary factors that determine the value range for rendering an object:

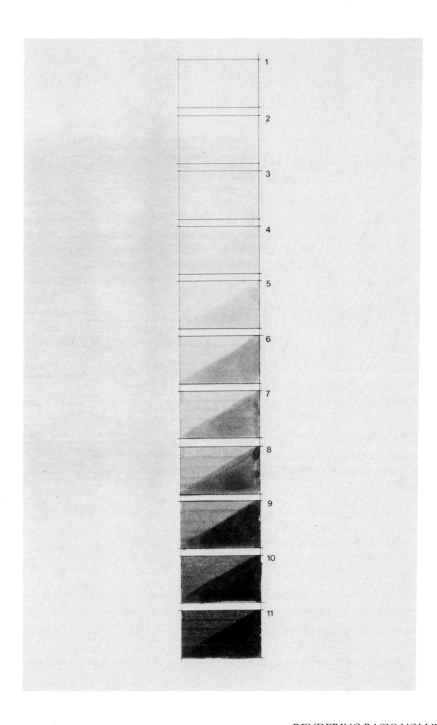

1. The intensity and directness of the light. Direct, strong light (i.e., sunlight) will wash out one surface and create a dark shade side and a harsh shadow. For this lighting situation a wide range of values will be needed. A brightly lit room with light walls will bounce so much light around that the contrast between the highlight surface and the shade side will be much less and a narrow range of values will be needed. As the intensity of light decreases, the values will become darker, and there will be less contrast. Therefore, a narrower and darker range of values will be needed.

2. The color of the object. Dark objects require a dark range of values, while light objects require a light range of values.

   Using a white cube as an example, we can see how different light conditions create different value ranges:

light condition	value range
direct/bright	1, 2, 3, 4, 5, 6
diffused/bright	1, 2, 3
direct/dim	2, 4, 6, 7
diffused/dim	4, 5, 6

For a dark object, even a black one, the range will be the same, but chosen from the dark (black) end of the scale.

3. Reflectiveness of an object. This does not so much affect the value range as the contrast. A very shiny object will pick up and reflect light from the surrounding objects. Therefore, dark, reflective objects will have some very light reflections in them.

The problem, then, is to determine which surfaces are light and dark and how light to make them. For this we assume that most objects are hit by strong, fairly direct light such as sunlight, and assign relative values to each surface.

4-4. The gray scale shown here was made with cool gray markers. Each rectangle shows both a single and a double coat of marker. You can see how much of the shading done in rendering can be achieved with multiple layers of the same marker, rather than by changing markers.

To do this a simple analysis of the amount of light striking each surface can be made. If we simplify light by making a series of parallel lines, the greater the number of lines per inch that strike a surface, the lighter the value (figure 4-5). Naturally, the lightest areas will then be where the light rays are perpendicular to the surface. This occurs at corners and edges that face the light. Therefore, they have highlights. Surfaces where light is at a very oblique angle will be dark. From this analysis, we can assign relative values to the surfaces of an object. By convention, the edges have highlights, the top surface is light, the front surface is a middle value, and the back surface is dark or perhaps in shade.

Basic Volumes Showing Light and Shadow

The accompanying examples analyze some basic volumes and simple products. The number system refers only to the order of values from light to dark and does not refer to a specific brand of marker. You should note that since the shadow area is only the lack of direct light on the floor or ground surface, it is not totally dark. Therefore, it is not black and may often be lighter than the shade side of a dark object.

Reflected Light

Another source of light on an object is that which is reflected from surrounding surfaces. Since you are only rendering one object and do not see the source of the reflected light, you must assume some conventions about it.

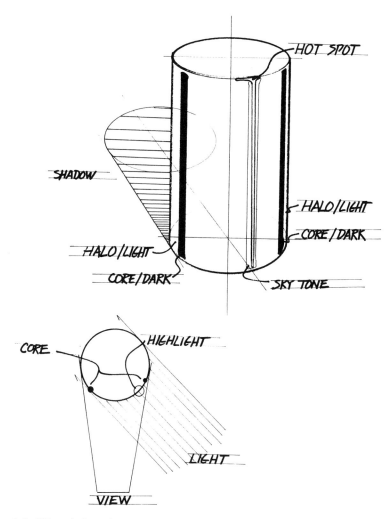

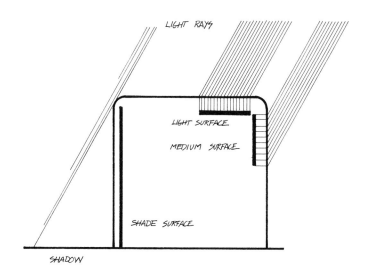

4-5. The more light that strikes the surface, the lighter in value that surface will appear. This diagram shows the most light striking the top surface; this is the most common situation.

4-6. Where light strikes a surface directly, there is a highlight or hot spot. Toward the edges the values become dark, and right at the edge is a halo of reflected light.

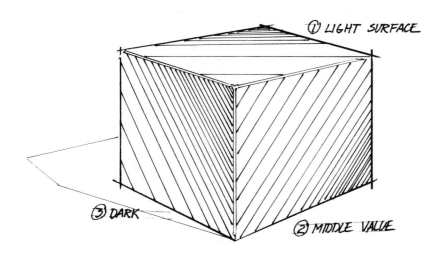

① LIGHT SURFACE

③ DARK

② MIDDLE VALUE

The most important aspect of reflected light is called a halo. This is light reflected from a background surface onto the shade side of an object (figure 4-6). It creates a slight glow on this dark side and also by contrast a dark "core" just before the edge. The halo not only gives a little extra light, but also reflects some color onto the shade area. This will be discussed later.

Surface Variation

Another convention of value is that a surface will not have only one flat value. The complexities of reflected light may be too involved to render, but they can be generalized by allowing for two to three values on a surface, moving from light to dark. The examples (figures 4-7 to 4-9) show how to apply this convention to some basic volumes.

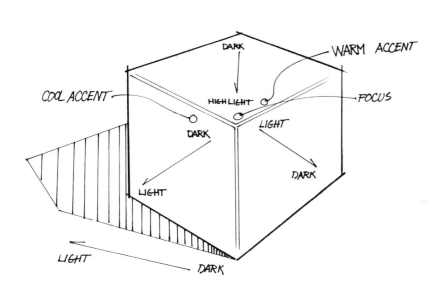

COOL ACCENT

DARK — WARM ACCENT

HIGHLIGHT — FOCUS

DARK

LIGHT

DARK

LIGHT

LIGHT — DARK

4-7 and 4-8. In addition to different surfaces having different relative values, each surface will modulate from light to dark within its value range.

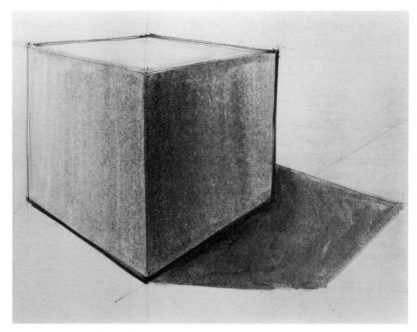

4-9. This quick sketch of a cube shows how markers can be used to modulate a surface. A dark-value marker was put on one edge and a lighter marker was used to blend it over the surface.

RENDERING BASIC VOLUMES AND SIMPLE OBJECTS

4-10. This photograph of a black plastic box shows the strong reflections of the cardboard on which it sits. Now that those reflections are almost horizontal.

4-11. The small clear box in this photograph illustrates how edges of transparent material tend to collect lights and darks. Note that the color of the black box when seen through the clear box is washed out and lighter.

Dull or Glossy Surfaces

The primary difference between dull and glossy surfaces is contrast. A dull surface has very low contrast because it diffuses the light that strikes it, and the values gradate softly. A glossy surface shows strong contrasts and tends to isolate value areas rather than to gradate them. Another aspect of glossy surfaces is the way that they reflect other objects, shadows, and smaller parts (figure 4-10).

Transparent Materials

In order to convey a sense of a material's transparency, you must both show something through the material and show the transparent material itself. To do this, the elements seen through the material are modified by altering the color (usually making it lighter), and distorting the contours near the edges of the transparent material. To add the necessary mass to the transparent material, some color and value will be concentrated in flowing lines at the edges and corners (figure 4–11). Also some glare will appear on the frontal areas of the transparent surface that will block all vision through the material.

Reflections

When and where to use reflections are important considerations in rendering. Reflections are difficult and time-consuming to put in but are necessary for a convincing drawing (figures 4-12 to 4-14). There are two basic types of reflections: general and specific. A general reflection implies an unseen light source and is highly stylized. The most common general reflections are the horizon line, a reflection of the object itself onto an implied floor or ground, and light reflections on the top of the object. Specific reflections are small elements reflected back onto the product. They reflect their full size in perspective and are rendered with less intensity and a narrower value range than if they were actual objects.

These basic conventions and a number of more specific techniques are described and illustrated in the following portfolio of examples. They need to be practiced and understood before setting up a full rendering.

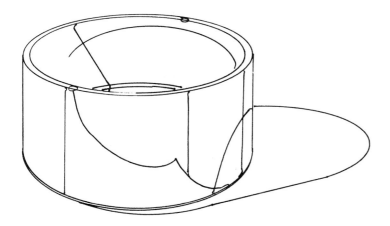

4-12. This line drawing shows where the highlights, shadows, and reflections are on a plastic bowl. This line analysis will serve as a guide for rendering the bowl.

4-14. This quick marker sketch of the bowl indicates the complexity of reflections possible in even a simple product. For effective rendering, most of these complexities would be eliminated in favor of more generalized reflections.

4-13. Notice how the straight edges of the cardboard are curved and pulled up in the reflection on the convex bowl surface.

RENDERING BASIC VOLUMES AND SIMPLE OBJECTS

Portfolio of Examples

Basic Reflections

The characteristics of a surface—whether it is flat or curved, glossy or dull—will determine the nature of reflections onto that surface. You want to put reflections typical to the kind of surface you are trying to describe into your rendering to make it believable. In the accompanying examples you will see how the basic volumes accept reflections. You should be able to apply this information to the rendering of your designed forms.

An important aspect of reflections is what happens at the transition points between surfaces; e.g., when a flat side changes to a corner radius on a product. Close attention at these points will help you render more convincingly and quickly. A gestured stroke may be started and ended appropriately to suggest these transitions. This eliminates the need for time-consuming detailing on sketches.

Once the nature of reflections is understood, they can be modified to simulate glossy or dull surfaces by the amount of contrast used to render them, the amount of reflected color, and the crispness of the reflections. Dull surfaces will reflect objects as a soft, vague, value change, while glossy surfaces will show a clear, harsh reflection. Also, as an object becomes lighter in color it will reflect more of the colors around it. Textured surfaces can be glossy or dull, and they tend to break up

reflections and segment them in the same pattern as the texture. (See C 5 in the color section.)

Surface Characteristics

As with a mirror, a flat reflective surface reproduces what is in front of it with the same spacing, size, and relative angle of the object to the reflective surface (figure 4-15). When rendering, this is all done in perspective, and the reflection is the "mirror image" of the object.

Once the basic reflection is penciled in, there are three considerations that will determine how to render it: first, whether the reflected object is light or dark; second, what color it is; and third, the gloss and texture of the reflective surface. Dark and brightly colored objects reflect clearly and strongly on light surfaces, and light objects reflect strongly on dark surfaces.

The color of the reflected object is also reflected onto the rendered surface. If the rendered surface has strong color itself, the reflected color will only tone it, usually warm (yellow or pink) or cool (blue or violet). If the rendered surface is a soft or neutral color (yellow, for example), blue reflected onto it will create a bluish green reflection.

The final consideration is the gloss and texture of the rendered surface. A glossy surface reflects a very clear image with strong color while a dull surface has a vague reflection, low in contrast with only a tonal color change. Texture seems to fragment a reflection and dissolve it around the edges.

Curved Surfaces

Like mirrors at a fun house, curved surfaces tend to condense or expand reflections (figure 4-16). A flat surface "sees" or faces an

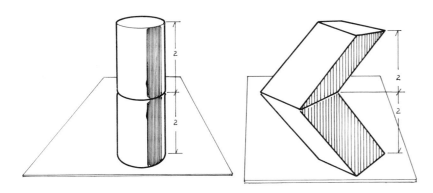

4-15. Flat reflective surfaces are mirrorlike and reflect objects in equal perspective size and at an equal angle.

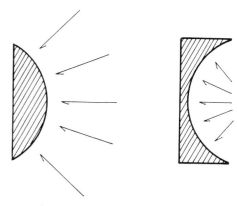

4-16. Convex surfaces will condense reflections, while concave surfaces will expand reflections.

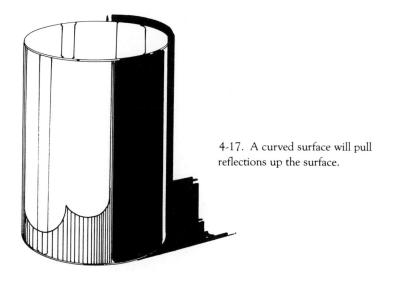

4-17. A curved surface will pull reflections up the surface.

environment equal to its size and reflects one to one. A convex surface opens up to the environment and sees more than its size. Thus it condenses the reflections to fit them all on its surface. A concave surface, on the other hand, closes up on itself and "sees" a smaller environment than its size. Thus it expands reflections to fill the surface.

The most common curved volume is convex—a cylinder. Naturally, the reflections are condensed, but something else happens as well. The further the reflected object moves away from the cylinder, the more its reflection is "pulled up" the surface (figure 4-17). Because of the curve of the cylinder, all points of an object get progressively further away. Hence, the reflection curves up the cylinder in a parabola. This tendency of reflections to pull up a curve is helpful when rendering cylinders. By pulling highlights and values in the direction of the cylinder, an illusion of a curved surface is created (figures 4-18 and 4-19). Depending upon

4-18. This marker sketch shows reflections being pulled up the surface, as well as a large core area that gives the cylinder some gloss. Because of the moderate level of contrast, the cylinder does not appear brightly reflective.

4-19. This cylinder shows a typical metal top surface. It has a broad, pie-shaped highlight, at almost a right angle to which is a thin sympathetic highlight. The rest of the top is a medium to dark value.

how much detail and contrast are used in the reflection, the surface will appear glossy or dull. On a cone the same pulling of reflections occurs, but, as expected, the reflections are pulled toward the tip of the cone (figure 4-20).

Concave surfaces on volumes and products are rare. They are usually found only on an inside corner. They expand reflections, but rather than pull them up the height of the curve, the reflections are drawn back toward the reflected product. In most cases expanding a highlight or dark reflection in a concave corner is all that is necessary.

Indicating reflections on these basic surfaces helps us see them as real. Reflections can be rendered very specifically as definite, identifiable objects, or in a generalized, generic manner. Since you are rendering objects that do not exist, it is helpful to select reflections that are either natural to the product, (from the expected environment), are from the background used in the rendering, or are conventional metaphors for reflections.

Glossy and Dull Surfaces

Glossy surfaces produce strong, crisp reflections. As a surface becomes duller, the reflections become more muted, vague, and lower in contrast. A number of conventions can be used to indicate reflections on both glossy and dull surfaces.

A stylized horizon line is reflected onto the side of a video product (figure 4-21) to show it as a glossy surface. Horizon lines are most commonly used when rendering outdoor products such as automobiles. However, the technique can also be employed on indoor products to suggest a table edge or the corner of a room. The horizon line consists of a crisp, high-contrast line drawn across the surface. From this line down to the bottom edge of the surface, the value gradually fades and becomes slightly lighter. On flat-topped surfaces, horizontal strokes indicate a dull finish. Stroking the marker in an almost vertical line toward the viewer gives a gloss to the surface (figures 4-22 and 4-23). Isolating a solid area of color on a surface and curving it into the edges of the

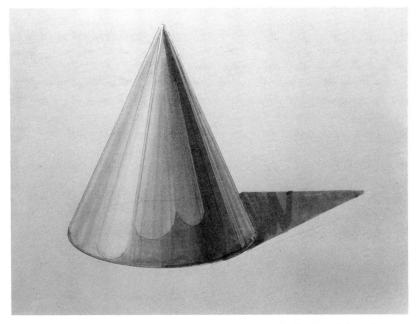

4-20. A cone is rendered in essentially the same way as a cylinder, but all the reflections taper to the peak and a highlight is located at the top.

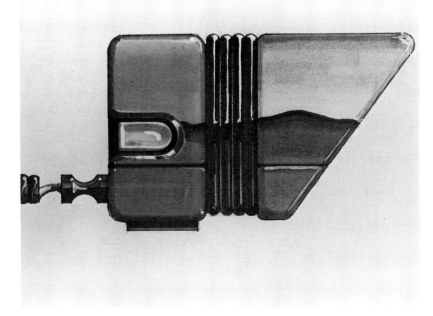

4-21. Concept Sketch, Paul Degenkalb. A stylized horizon line is reflected in the side of this product to show it as a glossy surface. Normally, horizon lines are only put on outdoor products such as cars.

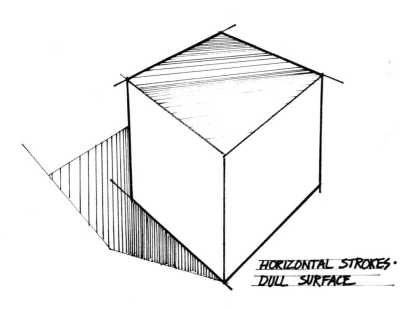

HORIZONTAL STROKES·
DULL SURFACE

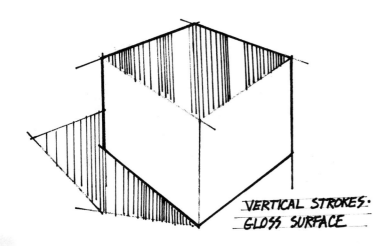

VERTICAL STROKES·
GLOSS SURFACE

surface, or rounding it into a puddle shape, works for curved surfaces. Often a small gestural distortion in the edge line of a solid area will add a sense of detail to a generalized reflection. A cylinder with a broad reflection by the highlight (figure 4-24) shows this gestural distortion—the strong contrast makes it glossy. A gradual change in values makes a dull surface (figure 4-25).

It is important to remember that most volumes are combinations of different surfaces. For example, a flat side will move into a curved corner. The reflection must make these transitions (figure 4-26). This is one reason why, at a rounded corner, the reflection from the flat surface will flow into the edge and run along the length of the rounded corner.

In addition to reflections, different materials are rendered differently because of their specific characteristics or manufacturing process. The materials also affect the reflections and how we render them.

4-22. Horizontal strokes on a top surface indicate a dull finish, while vertical strokes indicate a glossy finish.

4-23. By using dark markers, letting some white paper show, and using vertical strokes, this cube looks like a glossy black box. Each surface was masked so that the markers could be used freely while maintaining crisp edges.

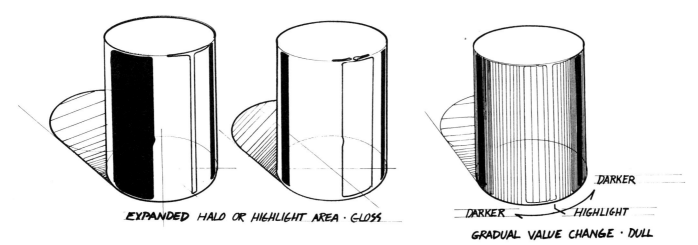

EXPANDED HALO OR HIGHLIGHT AREA · GLOSS

DARKER

DARKER — HIGHLIGHT

GRADUAL VALUE CHANGE · DULL

4-24. A broad highlight or core area on a cylinder gives a glossy surface. A gradual change in values makes a dull surface.

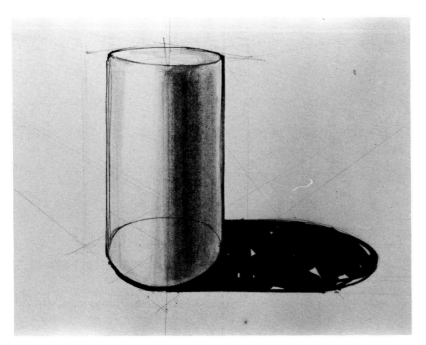

4-25. This cylinder is shown with a light, dull surface created by using light-value markers and little contrast.

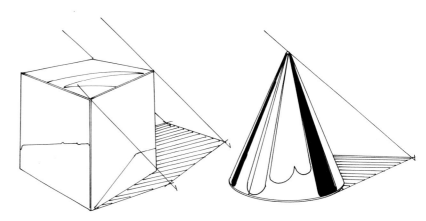

4-26. These two basic volumes show how the edge of a table is reflected onto them. On the cube the reflection is straight across the surface. On the cone the corner reflection is distorted and pulled up to the peak.

C-1. Motorcycle. The complexity of this product makes it much easier to render as a side view. The rendering emphasizes the reflections and highlights.

C-2. Truck Axle. This is a more illustrative use of markers. Each part of the product was rendered in a different hue to separate it clearly from the other parts. Shadows and highlights are still important; the brightest colors were reserved for the smaller parts, while dark or neutral colors were used for the larger parts.

C-3. Movie Camera, Mark Bonnette. This rendering clearly shows the form of the product. Bright highlights as well as strong contrasts can be seen on the surfaces. By exaggerating these elements the rendering has more impact and is more easily understood by the viewer.

C-4. Toy Train. The five hues used to make this sketch are shown to the right. You can see that a simple range from light to dark was needed for each color.

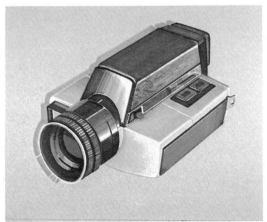

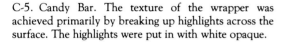

C-5. Candy Bar. The texture of the wrapper was achieved primarily by breaking up highlights across the surface. The highlights were put in with white opaque.

C-6. Computer Keyboard, detail. Even though the keys were handled quickly with a gestural stroke, shade, shadows, and reflections have all been indicated.

C-7. Adding Machine. The vents and parting lines have been indicated by shadows and highlights only. Attention is drawn to the working surface via color, contrast, and reflections.

C-8. Vase. The reflection of an imagined table corner is shown in the lower portion. The color scale to the right shows from top to bottom the media used. First, four values of blue marker were used to block out and render the basic form; two pencil colors were used to crisp up edges; two accent colors were put in to modify the dark areas; and a light gray was used to suggest a shadow. Finally, some white opaque was painted on for highlights.

C-9. Microwave Oven. Graphic elements may be applied over the marker surface using white ink in a Rapidograph pen or white opaque on a brush. The product is shown with the door open to emphasize the graphics on the control panel.

C-10. Color Wheel. The twelve hues were drawn with markers. Each hue shows the effect of both a single layer and a double layer of marker. To the right, the three primary colors are shown, each with two tints (above) and two shades (below). One hue with its tints and shades forms the basis of a color palette.

C-11. Automobile, Dennis Huguley. This is a good example of the type of rendering done in an automotive design studio. Because the basic forms are familiar and are the same for each rendering, a more exaggerated style can be developed and dramatic techniques employed. The highlights give a feeling of strong, direct light. There is also an abundance of reflected color toning the fender blue and the hood orange.

C-12. Horn. With the use of some white opaque for small reflections in the dark areas and for spot highlights, the rendering is complete.

C-13. C.B., George Tiston. The final detailing of the product was completed, including a simple background. Extensive highlight work was done with opaque and white pencil. Texture and typographic details were added with a fine-point brush, pencil, or pen. The paper color still serves as the middle value area.

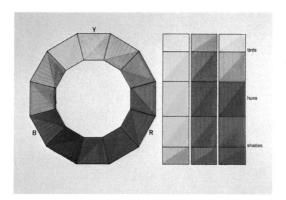

HUMAN FACTORS

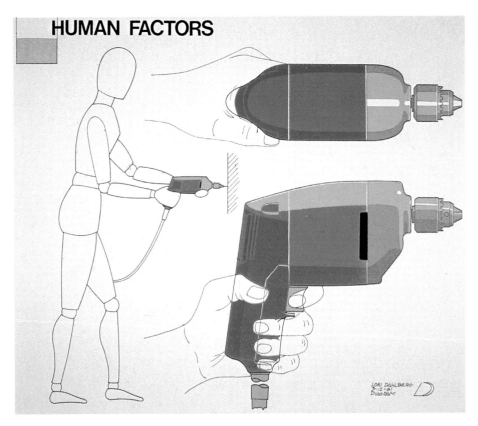

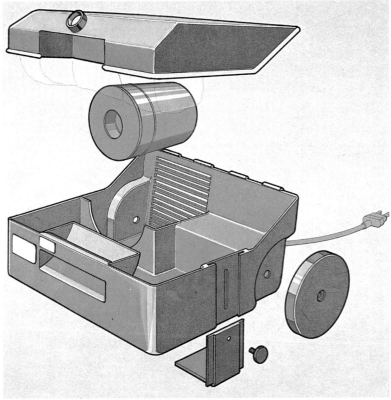

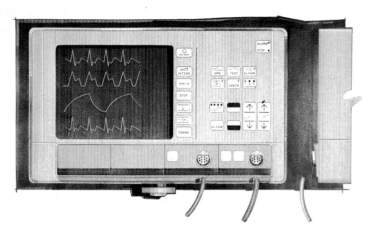

CONCEPT 1

C-14. Hand Drill, Lori Dalhberg. Transparent colored films make bold, bright renderings. Dark areas and lines must be drawn in before the films are put down. Highlights are easily cut in with an X-acto knife after the film is down.

C-15. Exploded View of a Product. Colored films are most effective on diagrams such as this where there is little detail that would require tedious cutting of the films. The flat, crisp colors also relate to the mechanical nature of diagrams.

C-16. Monitor, Jim Haager. This represents a more formal approach to presenting supporting information for a design concept. The orthographic views were rendered so that the design information reads well, yet there is very little technical information offered; this can be better supplied in the form of technical drawings or blueprints.

Wood

Rendering wood involves using a series of layers of marker color to build up color variations and subtle grain. Grain lines may be put in with a fine-point marker at the start of the rendering or may be added as final detailing with a Prismacolor pencil (figure 4-27).

A careful observation of the grain patterns and color variations common to wood is helpful before applying the markers, since color and grain pattern vary greatly in different woods. For small areas of wood a simple palette, consisting of a light brown marker, a dark brown marker, and a fine-point gray or brown pencil, is all that is needed. For larger areas a more extensive palette (up to five markers) is required, ranging from a light tan to a very deep brown. Some accent colors are also helpful. For woods like oak and maple, a yellow highlight marker and a deep reddish brown marker make good accents. For dark woods like walnut, a tan and a dark, blackish brown are good accents. When selecting a wood palette look carefully at the wood you want to render for the very light areas, the general tone of the wood (some are very red and others cool brown), and the dark areas. Then select a series of markers that moves through that range.

If possible, mask out the area to be rendered so that the markers may be applied quickly and freely. With a fineline waterbase marker draw in some grain lines, then stroke the lightest marker over the area, overlapping and leaving some streaks of white paper. Apply successive layers of progressively darker markers using the same technique, allowing some of the light marker to show through. The final piece should have a gradual change from light to dark across the surface, with the back third (i.e., the third furthest from the viewer) being darkest. The overlapping and gaps in the strokes create the color variations and suggest the grains of wood. The layering of markers blends the strokes and deepens the color for a rich, unified surface. Be careful not to overwork the surface or put in too many layers, as the paper will become saturated and muddy looking. When detailing the wood, add more grain lines and perhaps some reflections or glare. Light grain lines will "age" the wood, as will heavy dark lines. Rubbing a light pencil tone over part of the wood gives a luster to it and suggests a reflection.

When rendering wood products you are forced to work in the direction of the grain; otherwise the considerations for highlights, shade, and shadows are the same as with any product. Light and dark surfaces are achieved by using more or less of the light or dark wood colors from your palette. The only unusual area on wood is the endgrain. This is seldom seen in wood products and is easily rendered by using the blunt end of the marker and dabbing color on.

4-27. The three stages in rendering wood are shown to the left. On the right, from top to bottom, the wood itself is shown with a light grain, like new wood; as aged wood with both light and dark grain; and as planks by indicating joint lines.

Metals

The two important aspects of rendering metals are getting the color right and having the proper range of contrast in the marker colors chosen. Some metals are highly reflective and need strong contrasts while others are softly reflective, requiring a narrow range of marker contrasts. The most common metals—aluminum, chrome, and steel—are rendered in cool grays with a cool, light blue cast to them. Golden or yellow metals like bronze are rendered with a rich yellow, a light golden brown (or ochre), and a darker warm brown (figure 4-28). Dark metals have particular color casts to them. For example, copper needs a light pink for highlights and a medium and dark pinkish brown for the body and reflections.

Metals are usually polished to a very reflective gloss or brushed to a soft luster. These two effects are rendered very differently (figure 4-29).

4-28. Comparing the copper bottom of this pan to the steel top, you can see that the high-contrast handling of the markers is the same regardless of the color. Notice the slightly softer contrast on the handle to indicate plastic.

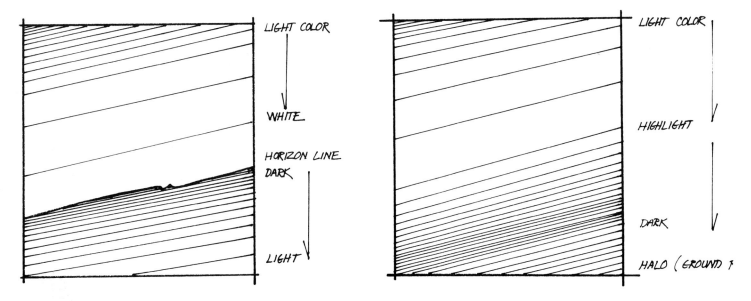

4-29. Two methods of rendering a flat metal surface are shown here. Both have a large light area and a dark section. For more reflective surfaces (left), a high contrast is set up between the light and dark areas; this is called a horizon line. For brushed surfaces (right) there is a gradual blending between the two areas.

Brushed Metals

Brushed, or soft, metals require blending of markers, allowing for a highlight area and a dark area. As with wood, masking off the area helps. A light range of colors (grays #1 through #4) is common for flat surfaces. Apply the lightest value over three-fourths of the area at a near-vertical slant (figures 4-30 and 4-31). Maintain the same slant and work quickly from light to dark markers, blending them so that there is a hint of streaking, but no definite marker lines. The final surface will have light streaks throughout and should have a broad light area in the upper third with the lower third relatively dark in value. You may have a tendency to make the surface too dark and overworked; watch out for this.

Where a surface changes levels or is bent, it is helpful to mask it off after about half the blending is done and finish working the main portion. Then go back to the masked area and put the darker values into it. In this way, the level changes will be more apparent since there will be both a pattern and value difference from the main surface.

After the basic surface is rendered, switches, knobs, readouts, and other details may be added. Most details can be put in with darker markers right over the "metal" surface. Large details can be rendered on separate paper, cut out, and glued in place. Very small light areas can be put in with a thin layer of white opaque watercolor and carefully tinted with a light marker stroke. The edges of the masked area will also need attention, usually given by highlighting the top and "front" edges (those closest to the highlight area) and darkening the back and bottom edges with a fineline dark gray.

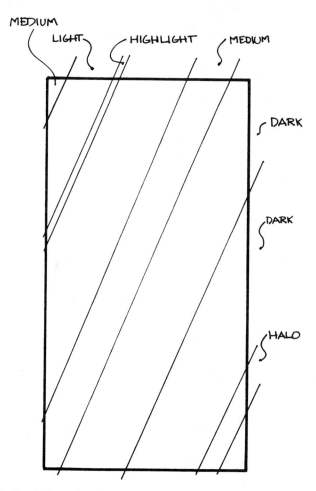

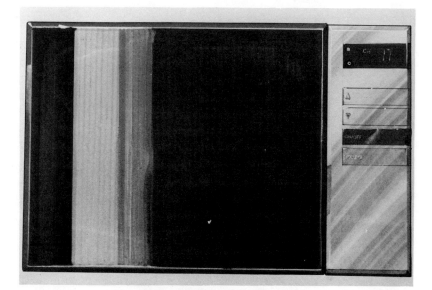

4-30. Brushed metal surfaces are stroked in a vertical pattern with little contrast on the surface.

4-31. The brushed metal surface on this control panel was achieved by blending light markers in almost vertical strokes. After the light markers were put down, details were added with dark markers and opaque white paint or chalk.

Glossy Metallic Surfaces

Glossy metallic surfaces are very different from satin-finish metals. They act like mirrors and reflect a great deal of both lights and darks. The scissors sketch (figure 4-32) shows how patterns of lights and darks gather on an irregular metal surface. In addition, rounded edges and curves are common when the metals are formed. This causes reflections to follow the curves or flow into the edges, very much as on a plastic surface. Metal has certain details that distinguish it from plastic, however. On the wagon (figure 4-33), for example, the ripples in the round overlip on the top of the sides and the thin grip are clues that the wagon is made of metal.

The colors used again depend upon the type of metal. For ease of rendering, the light and dark reflections are done in the metal colors without a lot of reflected color. There are some basic guidelines for developing a glossy surface, shown in the examples:

- Decide on a major dark reflection area and smaller "sympathetic" (similar) reflection area.

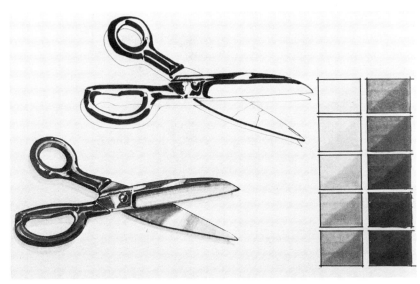

4-32. This scissors sketch shows how patterns of lights and darks can break up an irregular metal surface.

4-33. Painted Metal Wagon. When metal is painted, it becomes more difficult to distinguish from plastic. However, the ripples in the round overlip on the top of the sides and the thin handle grip are clues that the wagon is metal.

- Keep high contrasts between lights and darks. The light areas will carry the "color" of the metal so they will predominate. Avoid many middle values.
- Round or "flow" all edges and corners of the dark areas.
- Thin and draw out darks in tight edges. Let them thicken at corners.
- Reflect smaller parts onto the metal. Even a reflection may be reflected back onto another part.
- Modify the dark reflections slightly with more than one dark value.
- Tone down one edge of a dark area with a middle value. Leave the other edge strong.
- Keep the darks off the outside edge of the object. Halos belong there.

Some painted highlights and pale color may be added to the highlight areas to help pop the drawing. The detailing of parts and the addition of color elements finish the object and make it believable.

You will want to keep in mind the manufacturing processes metal products go through when rendering them. Stamped, formed metal typically has soft, round corners with wide highlights, while cut metals have sharp (hard) edges that pick up very fine, bright highlights.

Plastic

Plastic takes on almost any form, color, or texture, imitating any other material. There are some idiosyncrasies of plastic, however, that help to identify it in a rendering.

Being molded or heat-formed, most plastic objects have slight distortions or stress points that cause waves or wrinkles in the reflections, particularly in the highlights (figure 4-34). The surface distortions can be indicated by adding a small blip or wave to the major reflection. This is different from rendering metal, in which the marker strokes are kept crisp and straight. Stress points are found along edges and in corners. A slight wrinkle in the highlight is an effective device here (figures 4-35 to 4-37).

4-34. Telephone Concept Sketch, Mark Kurth. This marker sketch was done on brown-line diazo print paper. The broad highlight was distorted at the ends by the gesture stroke of the marker. This broad highlight and distortion is characteristic of plastics.

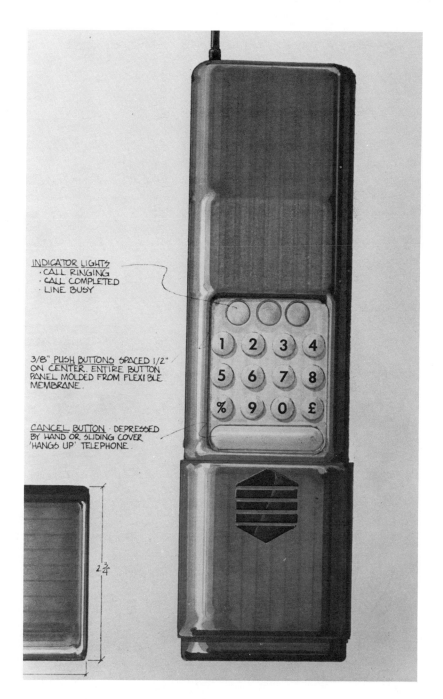

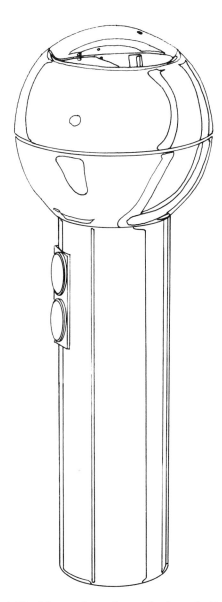

4-35. A line analysis of a simple plastic flashlight.

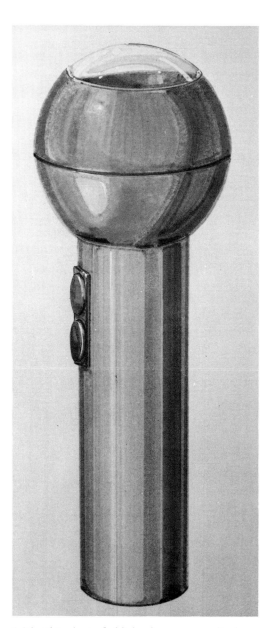

4-36. This plastic flashlight shows a generalized approach to reflections on both a cylinder and a sphere. In addition, the transparent lens distorts the back edge of the plastic.

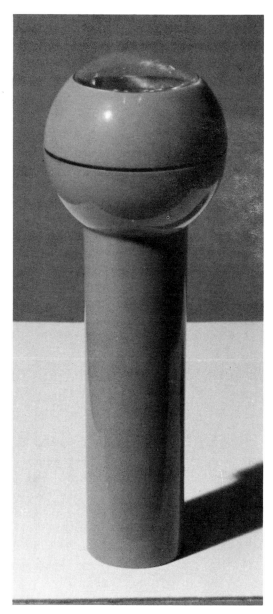

4-37. A photograph of the flashlight has more complicated reflections, but they are not necessary when the attention is to be drawn to the lens area.

The colors in plastic are often bright and deep. Plastic is also highly reflective. This strength of color and reflectiveness encourage subtle variations in the color, particularly in the highlight and shade areas (figures 4-38 and 4-39). For example, adding yellow to the highlight on a red object and violet to the shade area will give added depth and visual interest to your rendering.

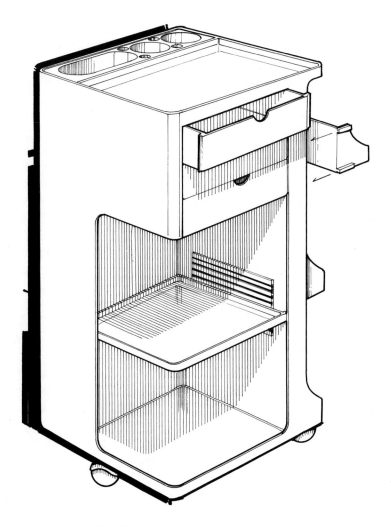

4-38. A line analysis of a plastic taboret.

4-39. Plastic Taboret. This monochromatic rendering may be considered a color sketch because of the limited use of color and reflections. It was done by masking out the product and vertically stroking in the markers, leaving a wide highlight on the leading edge. Darks were added to shelves to give depth, then highlights were put on the edges so they would stand out.

Glass and Transparent Plastics

Transparency is often considered the most difficult rendering problem, probably because you are asked to render what is behind the transparent object, rather than the object itself. There are three basic areas of consideration when rendering transparency: first, the structure of the object as seen in the edges and corners; second, reflections and glare on the surface of the material; and third, distortions of what is seen through the transparency (figure 4-40).

Wherever you can see the thickness of a transparent material (in the edges and corners) there will be a collection of lights, darks, and color.

4-40. Desk Light, George Simon. The textured glass in this light distorts whatever is seen through it. This helps to show its transparency as well as the texture of the glass.

With clear glass, the edges show a light, cool green. With plastic, the edges carry color or show white light. In the beer sign rendering (figure 4-41), white opaque was painted on to show the light in the edges and glare on the surface of the glass. In rendering a transparent object, then, be careful to indicate the thickness of the material at all edges and corners. Use light pencil guidelines and "flow" collected color and light lines through these edges. You will notice that wherever an edge of a transparent object crosses over a line behind it, that line is distorted and pulled along the edge.

Since all transparent surfaces are very smooth, there will be glare and strong highlights. Glare can be shown with a broad streak of white that blocks our view through the material. This glare is usually found on the surface facing the light source. Angling the glare stroke towards the viewer helps create the illusion of light being reflected toward him.

To indicate that we are looking through a transparent material, some slight distortions near the edges along with an offset of the background lines help. When looking through a curved glass, the background line will not only be offset, it will also be curved as though it were following the shape of the glass. Also, the intensity of the color and the crispness of line in the background may be reduced, particularly where more than one layer of transparency is covering the ground. The beer sign (figure 4-42) shows a shifting of the background when seen through the glass—it has been isolated from the edges of the glass, and white opaque was used to show the glass itself.

A final element that adds to the illusion of transparency is the reflection of environmental elements onto the object. This is rarely done in product rendering as it tends to confuse and unnecessarily complicate the rendering. However, putting these reflections in windows and doors adds nice minor details to architectural rendering. Because these reflections are somewhat transparent and you can see through them to the background, using colored pencils over the markers is the simplest way to render them.

There are cases in which transparent materials act more as mirrors than as windows. When the far side of the transparency is an enclosed dark space, such as the interior of a car, the transparency may be mirrorlike. When the far side is light, we see through the transparency. This is helpful when rendering buildings. In the daytime, buildings are relatively dark inside and light is mirrored off the windows. Therefore,

4-41. Beer Sign, Thomas A. Schutz Co. The glass in this rendering was put in with white opaque.

4-42. Beer Sign, detail, Thomas A. Schutz Co. In addition to the white opaque, the isolation of background color away from the edges of the glass helps give the illusion of transparency.

we see reflections of the sky, trees, and other buildings. As we get closer to the building, more outside light is blocked by other buildings and the ground, and we begin to see into the windows. At night, when more light is coming from within the building, we see through the windows.

Small areas of transparent material like the "windows" on calculator readouts offer little opportunity for elaborate reflections. Being aware of the edges and allowing for a minor soft glare is about all that is needed or wanted here. We are so accustomed to the transparent covers on readouts that rendering them is almost unnecessary.

Transparent materials that are tinted will tend to neutralize both the colors seen through them and what is reflected onto them. Neutralizing a color is done by pushing it toward the gray or brown ranges. Dark transparent materials can usually be rendered using warm gray markers with some colored pencil work added to liven up the grays.

Textured Surfaces

Textured surfaces are found in all types of materials. With mass production these textures are uniform and consistent. Because of this we can render them by detailing the texture in one focal area and generalizing its color and reflective quality over the rest of the surface, since we understand it will be uniformly reproduced throughout the surface.

Most textures have a definite pattern to them, usually a grid. This underlying structure must remain intact even with the most casual gestural treatment; otherwise the rendered texture becomes unreadable. It is easy to be lazy and try to gesture the entire surface without planning for the pattern of the texture. A simple way to avoid this is to lightly pencil in the textural pattern as a quick guide for the marker strokes and selected detailing.

4-43. To show a sense of light on this teddy bear, a light marker was dabbed on, then darker markers were dabbed on toward the shade area.

4-44. Teddy Bear, detail. Markers were dabbed to create the effect of nap on this toy bear.

To build up most textures, begin with a pale value of the material color and fill in the highlight areas. Next, work in the medium values and finally the dark, or shade, values. To show a sense of light on the teddy bear in figures 4-43 and 4-44, for instance, a light marker was dabbed on to show both the nap and highlight areas. Darker markers were dabbed on in the shade and shadow areas. Now go back into the drawing with a dark fine line and define specific details concentrating on one focal area, usually near the leading edge of the rendering. Complete the texture with white or light-colored chalk or pencil to define highlights across the surface. Again, concentrate on the focal area. Another way to get soft texture is to rub powdered chalk over the surface (figure 4-45), using two or three values for modeled surfaces. Then, use a soft eraser to create highlights. This technique works well with lightly colored papers, as the highlights do not become bright white.

The detailed textured pattern should gradually dissipate as it moves out of the focal area. The majority of the surface will be handled as a generalized gestural pattern, showing light and dark values but no specific details.

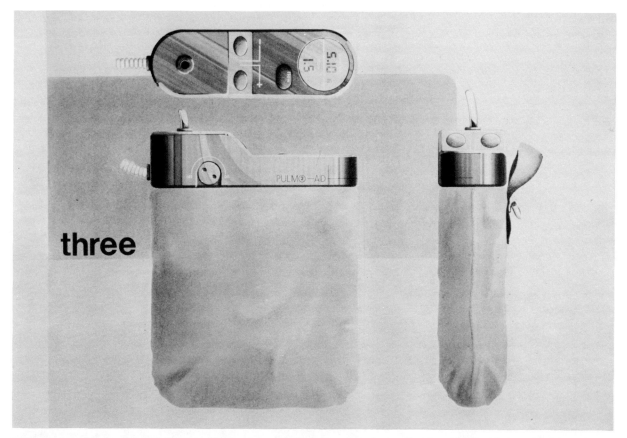

4-45. Air bag Concept, George Simons. Chalk over colored paper was used to render this soft, flexible bag. The bag area was masked out and powered chalk was rubbed on. A soft eraser was then used to pick out highlights.

Small Parts

This next set of examples deals with details and small parts of a product. Rendering small parts is no different from rendering larger forms except that, because they are small, less time is spent on them. A simple gestured stroke should be mastered to "drop in" these parts and details. (Refer to the buttons and switches in figures 4-46, 4-47, and 4-50.)

These detail parts are affected by lighting in the same way as are larger forms. Therefore, the gestured strokes must not only show the form of the part, but also indicate the light striking it. Consistent light and shadow will make these parts "read" more easily and fit the larger form better.

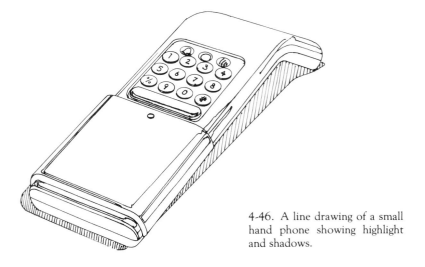

4-46. A line drawing of a small hand phone showing highlight and shadows.

4-47. Quick Sketch of a Portable Phone. The buttons were outlined with a thin line and a quick gesture of dark shade was put in along with small highlights. This is often all that is needed for minor details.

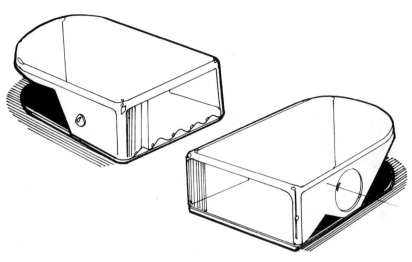

4-48. A line analysis of two small clips.

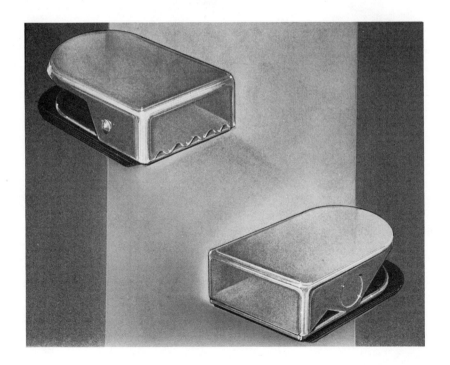

Knobs, Switches, Buttons

These parts usually have a flat or slightly rounded top surface that can be gestured in with a simple stroke. The stroke will vary slightly depending on whether the surface is flat, concave, or convex, but essentially it indicates a shade side leaving a white highlight. The body of the part can be reduced to a light, or highlight, side and a dark shade value. (See figure 4-50 and C6 in the color section.) An important element in rendering a knob, switch, or button is the threshold.

The threshold is the place where the part joins the body of the product. There is a slight gap at this point, and it should be carefully and accurately delineated with a dark fine line. Once this basic marker work is done, go back into the part and add any fine linework necessary to clarify the exact shape of the part or its texture. The final task is to put in highlights—a major highlight on the top leading edge, and a sympathetic highlight directly across from it on the top back edge. This technique of sympathetic highlights is useful and works in many situations. To pop the part off the surface, put a light shadow and perhaps a reflection of the part onto the surface of the product.

Vents, Parting Lines, Grilles

These details can be categorized as elements that are cut into the body of the product. As such they are all treated in the same manner: a dark line represents the opening, followed by a very thin medium-value line showing the thickness of the material around the cut. (See C7 in the color section.) Finally, a highlight runs along the furthest edge of the opening.

These vents and grilles are usually arranged in a pattern. To put spot highlights on them, draw a light line across the vents, suggesting the contour of the surface and spot highlights with white opaque on the highlight edge. There are two common types of vents—slots and circular holes. Both are handled in the same manner, but you must be careful to lay them out accurately to get even spacing.

4-49. Two Small Clips, David Skinner. Linework was used to describe the details on these small clips, often done with white to suggest highlight edges.

4-50. The buttons on this computer are important details, so they were fully rendered.
The housing for the computer was done in a minimal way since it is not a focal point.

Wires, Tubes, Cords

Linear elements, such as wires, tubes, and cords, are a simple matter when they are straight. A light value over the entire surface, a dark value to one side, and a highlight drawn down the length, just off center, are all that is needed. A hot spot and a thin line of reflected color through the length make good finishing touches.

When the elements are curved they become much more difficult to render; careful construction is required. A flexible curve or a rigid french curve is used to get a consistent curve and width of the part. Then ellipse guides are used along the length to maintain the proper circular cross section of the part. Once the light-line drawing is constructed, the markers are applied and fineline detailing is added to establish the exact contour. Wires and cords are often omitted from renderings because of the time it takes to render them well. An alternative to omitting them is to render the sections close to the product and suggest the remainder of the cord or wire with light lines, letting it fade out.

Lights and Lenses

Lights and lenses are fairly simple to render when they are small. A light value, or color, is used for the center; a medium value is used over the rest of the surface; then a dark value is applied at the outer edges (figure 4–51). The light center value may be put in first with a marker or added last by laying a light marker over white pencil or opaque. On some papers, colored chalk can be used to put in bright spots.

Larger lights present more of a problem. The lens often has a textured pattern to diffuse the light, and usually has a large reflector behind it. The patterned glass breaks up both the dark reflections and the highlights that the reflector has collected. By lightly penciling in the

pattern as a guide, the reflections and highlights can be loosely put down in a disjointed approximation of the lens pattern. The final detailing consists of some color linework on the lens to clarify the pattern and heavier dark linework around the edges (where a parting line would be) to clean up the rough appearance.

The examples in the portfolio section can be generalized to fit most product rendering situations. You are trying to imitate the effect of light on the surface of a product in rendering. This requires that you always keep in mind where the light source is and look for places where shadows and reflection can be used to enhance the rendering. Without this your renderings will appear dull and uninteresting.

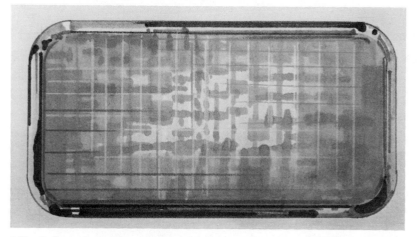

4-51. Reflector Lens. The pattern of the glass in this lens was shown by applying the markers in a regular pattern. Lightening the markers toward its center makes the lens seem to glow a bit.

CHAPTER FIVE

Setting Up a Rendering

Subject Selection

We can classify products into categories of relative complexity: simple objects, compound objects, and complex objects. We can also select a view to represent a product that either simplifies the rendering of it (an orthographic view) or makes it more complicated (a perspective view).

Since we experience objects from all sides, a perspective view appears the most natural and gives us the best understanding of the form. A perspective view shows more than one side of an object, and for most products, two or more sides are necessary to understand the form completely. Whenever possible use a carefully chosen perspective view for a presentation rendering. For certain objects and situations, however, an orthographic view is all that is needed; this is much quicker to draw and render.

When drawn in orthographic view, most simple cylindrical products (flashlights, hair blowers, and cookware, for example) show us the basic shape, which implies the form, as well as the proportions and scale

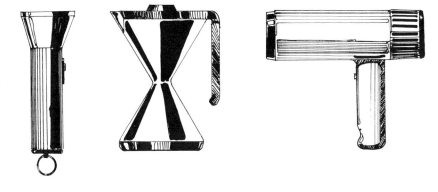

5-1. Orthographics of cylindrical products showing highlights and shade areas.

(figure 5-1). By using an orthographic view, the difficulty of rendering ellipses and other problems of perspective are eliminated. The drawing may be set up using actual scale dimensions and the markers quickly applied.

96

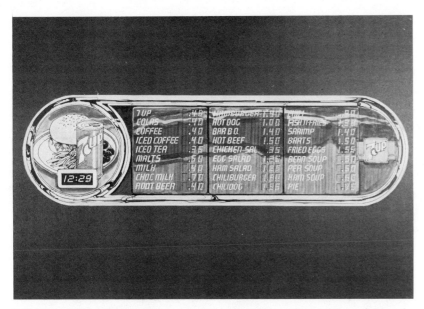

Products such as signs or television sets that have only one primary surface (i.e., surface of visual interest) and are essentially in low relief (flat) also lend themselves to orthographic rendering. Because these objects are not always cylindrical, a simple side view helps explain the form. Again, lay out the rendering by drafting the product as you would an architectural elevation, in full-scale whenever possible. Some products that work well for elevation (orthographic) renderings are television and stereo control panels, pocket calculators, display signage, and surfaces that are heavy with typographic elements (figures 5-2 to 5-4).

5-2. Menu Signage Board, Thomas A. Schutz Co. This orthographic rendering of a restaurant sign shows how flat objects with typography may easily be rendered without using perspective. This rendering also illustrates the free use of marker and the high contrast used to render the chrome trim. The loose, almost sketchy, application of marker is common to display and exhibit rendering.

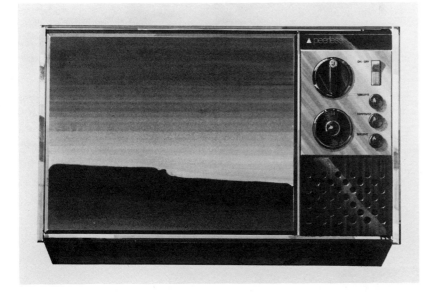

5-3 and 5-4. Orthographic Rendering of a Television with Side View. Two things to note in these renderings are the use of a reflected horizon line in the picture tube cover and the highlights running across the vents and speaker area. Some people find the use of a reflected horizon line too dramatic and prefer a more generalized, toned-down reflection.

Simple Objects

Simple objects are those that have one basic geometric form (i.e., a cylinder or cube), a minimal number of components and details such as knobs, parting lines, and readouts, and are of a single material with a simple texture or surface. These objects are usually unifunctional. Some examples of simple objects are bottles, flashlights, toasters, glassware, cooking utensils, and desk accessories. These simple objects are the easiest to draw as we have to understand only one basic volume. The effects of light on their surfaces are easy to achieve since there are few details to interrupt the application of the marker color. (See figure 5-5 and C8 in the color section.)

Compound Objects

Compound objects usually consist of a combination of two or more geometric forms. They have a limited number of smaller components and details (knobs, buttons, trim, and so forth) and usually exhibit two or more material types and textures. These products often offer a number of slight variations in their prime functions. Typical examples are television sets, furniture, blenders and other appliances, outboard motors, typewriters, and simple cameras. With the increased complexity of the perspective construction and the number of details on the surface that make a more complicated set of reflections and highlights, both the set-up and the marker application become more time-consuming and demanding.

Three steps in the rendering of a microwave oven are shown in figures 5-6, 5-7, and 5-8.

1. A line drawing was made with heavy line weights, to be used as an underlay for the rendering (figure 5-6).
2. A straightedge and felt-tip pen were used to correct perspective mistakes and tighten up the line drawing (figure 5-7).
3. Marker paper was put over the line drawing to render the product (figure 5-8). In this case a paper mask was put down around the control panel before the markers were applied. The markers could then be applied quickly and blended together. A gold pencil was used to locate the controls before the marker was put down. This metallic pencil shows through the dark marker, making it easy to see where the controls are located. (See also C-9 in the color section.)

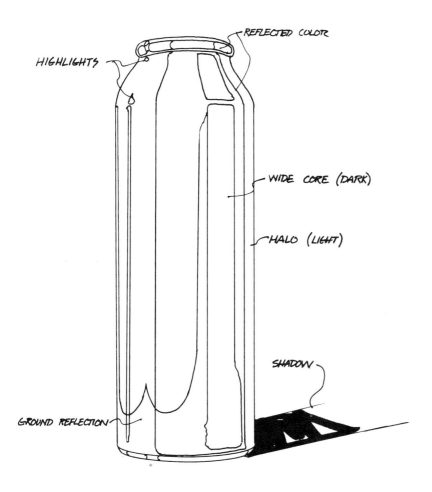

5-5. Simple line analysis of light and reflections on a vase.

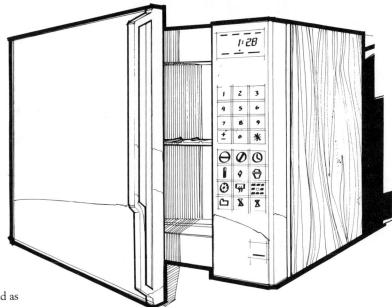

5-6. Line drawing with heavy line weights used as an underlay for a rendering.

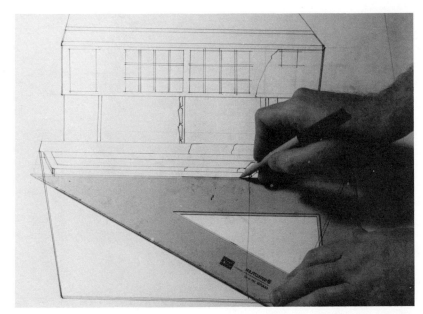

5-7. A triangle and felt-tip pen were used to tighten up this line sketch of a microwave oven.

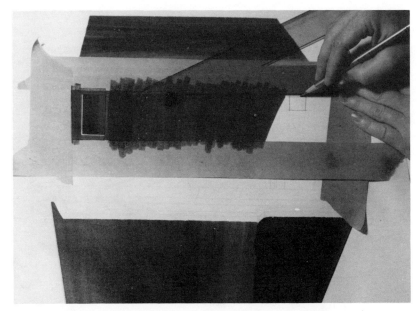

5-8. A paper mask was put around the control panel before putting down the markers. The markers could thus be applied quickly and blended together. A gold pencil was used to locate controls before the marker was put down. The metallic pencil shows through the dark marker, making it easy to see where the controls are located.

Complex Objects

Complex objects are made up of a number of simple and compound objects or have great intricacies of detail and surface variation. They often contain several material types and textures and a profusion of components and details. Some examples are: automobiles, 35-mm cameras, buildings, interiors, and boats. Because of the complicated and subtle changes in the surface of these objects, great familiarity with them and an easy, facile control of the rendering technique are required in order to render them convincingly. In addition to the relative complexity of an object because of form, number of details, and the choice of view in which to render it, more complex objects also have more intricate reflections and highlights. A line drawing of a complex object, such as that shown in figure 5-9, can be made simpler by using dark vignettes to shape the form and show the pattern of the buttons, rather than using fine linework to detail each one. The complexity of a computer terminal (figure 5-10) is in the keyboard. Showing each

button, its shadow, and its reflection, is time-consuming but necessary. However, the housing may be left almost unrendered, as there is little visual attention focused there.

All of these intricacies must be understood in terms of the visual metaphors needed to render them. Therefore, it is best for beginners to select simple objects for practice rendering and to build up to more complex objects as their skills progress.

Subject Analysis

When learning to render it is helpful to work from product photographs, from life, or to copy other product renderings so you will be able to see the values, reflections, and details that are necessary to make a rendering work. Once you have an understanding of the visual nature of these elements it becomes much easier to produce convincing render-

5-9. Line drawing using dark vignettes to block out form and show pattern of buttons.

5-10. Computer Terminal. This rendering concentrates on the suggestion of buttons and screen, leaving the housing almost unrendered. Shadows and reflections help make the buttons seem real.

ings of your own design concepts. Regardless of the source, it is essential that you get sufficient information about values, light source, materials, parting lines, form, controls, and other details in order to render the object. Otherwise you will have to invent these elements. To acquire this information you must make a careful analysis of the subject.

Subject analysis is usually done in the form of a series of thumbnail sketches or value studies that help establish the composition and set down the organization of visual elements. However, when working from a photograph much of the analysis can be done on the image itself. When I refer to working from a photograph I do not mean that you must copy the exact photographic image. The photograph may have the basic form you wish to render or show specific reflections you want in your rendering. The photograph is then used as a guide for rendering your own design.

Drawing from a Photograph

Magazines, brochures, and catalogs are sources of product photographs. However, it takes time and careful selection to find good ones. There are many more inappropriate and unusable photographs than there are useful ones, the main reason being that advertising a product (via a magazine photo) and trying to communicate the form and function of a product (via a rendering) present very different problems and result in different types of imagery. Once you have a selection of photographs you may wish to categorize them by subject and create a *morgue file*. This morgue file, or collection of photographs, can then be used as a ready source of visual information. (For example, a morgue file of chrome parts will provide information for rendering shiny surfaces.)

The first step in selecting a good photograph to work from is to evaluate the view of the product. Be sure you can see the whole object, not just the main part, and avoid dramatic, distorted, or exaggerated images, as they lose their credibility when rendered. Remember that the distortion and creative license allowed in photography are of a different nature than those employed in drawing; the two should not be unwittingly confused.

The photograph should be clear enough to enable you to identify the materials and understand the details. This usually means a large photograph without dark shadows or anything obstructing a portion of the view of the product. You may understand the product by mentally filling in the vague or obstructed areas. For rendering, however, you should be able to see and analyze the entire surface.

Once you have selected a clear photograph to work from, make a light pencil outline of the object on your paper. This may be done by sketching and refining, tracing, enlarging on a lucy graph (a tracing machine that allows you to enlarge or reduce an image), or any other method with which you feel comfortable. Now you must analyze the photograph and transfer the information about light and value onto your line drawing while correcting for photographic distortion and special lighting effects.

Most photographs will have multiple light sources. You need to find the primary light source and ignore the others. The most desirable direction for light to strike an object is over one of the viewer's shoulders. You will want to indicate with a simple, light pencil outline the highlight areas on your line drawing. The rough line drawing (figure 5-11) shows how highlights have been positioned on the form.

You must also be concerned with the value range and relative contrast of the object—the difference between the lightest and darkest values on the main body of the object. To analyze the value range, compare the

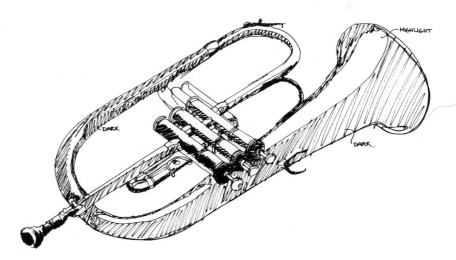

5-11. Rough line drawing used to determine form and work out highlights for a rendering.

photograph to your marker value scale. Then, with a fine black pen, carefully outline the areas of consistent value on the surface of the photograph. Wherever the values gradate you will have to make a decision as to where to break down the gradated section into a few flat value areas. Once you have the values outlined, transfer this information to your drawing page with light pencil outlines. Pay particular attention to the edges of these value areas. The more reflective the surface, the more the values "flow" into the edges of the object. A word of caution: most people tend to reduce the contrast of an object when the opposite should be done. Exaggerate the contrast range for your rendering. This helps to express the basic form of the object and makes the drawing hold up well when viewed from a short distance.

Another correction that must be made when working from a photograph is to adjust for camera distortion and make the line drawing fit conventional two-point perspective. Usually this requires only a straightening of all vertical lines so that they are parallel to each other and perpendicular to the bottom edge of the drawing paper. If photographic distortions are dramatic or exaggerated, it is probable that the photographer is exploiting photographic distortion for visual impact. It

is best, then, to select another photograph as you will have to completely reposition and redraw the object to correct it for rendering.

The final steps in analysis are to eliminate special photographic effects, such as reflected colored lights, and to understand the reflections so you may choose the ones that will make sense in your rendering. A photograph may seem very complicated to render because of the reflections. By making a careful line drawing, such as that shown in figure 5-12, the object becomes easier to understand. You can add only the highlights and reflections you feel are important and ignore the complexities of the photograph.

It takes time and experience to be able to interpret reflections and determine what causes them. Try to develop a habit of seeing the surface of objects in life and notice what causes the reflections on them. Luckily, in photographs, and more so in renderings, the reflections are generally simple and few; you just need practice in understanding them. After eliminating the special effects and selecting the major reflections, transfer this information to your line drawing. Now you should have a very light pencil-outline drawing that may look something like a paint-by-number layout without numbers. Using the photograph as a reference you are ready to apply the markers.

Drawing from Life

The major advantages in drawing from life are that you can see what causes highlights and reflections and manipulate the environment to get a composition with the visual effects you want. Some time spent in setting up a good still life will make the rendering go much more easily. The disadvantage in drawing from life is that you cannot compare marker value or color with the object as you can with a photograph. You must also be more discerning in observing details, particularly reflections and highlights. We have a tendency to overlook these visual phenomena in real life.

Once you have selected an object to draw, place it in a field or environment that will determine the reflections and set up a major light source (over one shoulder). To make the field as neutral as possible, place the object on a large sheet of paper that is not too bright in color. (Use white, brown, beige, or black.) This will give you only the basic reflections and make the object's surface easier to understand. Later you may wish to place the object on a split field of light and dark and

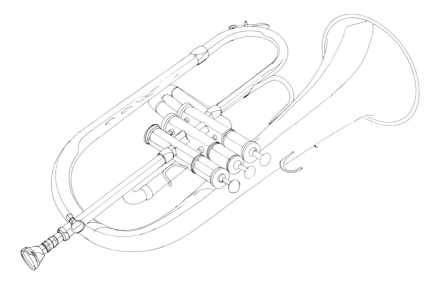

5-12. Tight line drawing made with ellipse guides and a flexible curve to be used as an underlay for a rendering.

position the dark area to reflect onto one side of the object. This will increase your contrast a little bit and show stronger reflective surfaces.

The next step in setting up a still life is positioning the major light source. This should be the strongest light to strike the object and should come from a seemingly neutral position. This light source will determine major and minor highlights, the intensity of reflections, and the shadows on the surface of the object as well as on the ground. A positionable lamp or floodlight works well for this. General room lights are usually too diffused and not strong enough to overpower ambient or other indirect light.

It is a good idea to reposition your still life until you get a pose that you like and understand. You may find that by holding neutral cards (the backs of pads) beside an object you can both create and delete reflections. This is a good technique for understanding how the room and environment are reflected on an object's surface, allowing you to decide what to include or leave out of the rendering. You are mainly interested in the reflections and shadows made by the object on itself and those basic reflections from the immediate environment that seem to relate to the object and help show the nature of the surface (glossy or textured). Whenever possible include the object being reflected in your rendering. This is difficult to do in most product renderings, and it is common to draw in only a simple background in addition to the product itself. Once the still life is arranged and understood, value studies need to be made to plan the drawing.

Drawing From Sketches

While the experiences of rendering from a photograph or from life teach us a lot about how to render, the ultimate goal of learning to render is to be able to communicate a design concept convincingly as a viable product. Since there are no photographs of product ideas to draw from, you will be working from rough thumbnail sketches. Almost all of the visual information needed to render the product must come from an intellectual analysis applied to a perspective layout.

Initially, you will need complete and accurate information about the proposed product. From your thumbnails, develop some rough-dimensioned orthographics (you will also need these to set up the perspective). These will help you accurately determine and understand the basic form of the product. The act of drawing the orthographics also makes you aware of, and forces you to make decisions about, such things as corner radii, switch positions, and parting lines.

One of the most common problems in concept rendering is the lack of convincing detail and functional necessities for a product. A technique for guarding against this is to make a list of all the details from a similar product. Consider what the product is made of; how it is controlled; the manufacturing process; how it is serviced; what it does; and note how these considerations affect the form (e.g., glossy plastic surface with rounded corners, series of push buttons on a slanted front plate, two-piece housing with parting line around the sides, removable battery plate). Be sure all of these details are accounted for in your design before you begin to render. This does not mean you must copy what has been done before, but rather that you account for the complexities of a real product and make your own decisions about the physical form they will take in your product. (Do not, however, copy a switch, for example, simply because it exists on another product. It may be unnecessary in your design or be changed to a different control element, such as a dial.)

Once you have sufficient information about the physical nature of your product you can begin the job of analyzing the visual qualities in order to render it. For this you will need to make a perspective layout of the new product on which you will lightly pencil in highlights, reflections, and details.

Try to see the product as a composition of basic geometric volumes. Determine a major light source and assign values to all the surfaces. Continue to work with this light source and lightly pencil in the major highlights. Be sure they are all oriented toward the light source. Next cast shadows from small elements of the object (e.g., switches) onto the surface.

The final step is to determine where you want reflections and what they will look like. For this it is very helpful to refer to a morgue file of photographs and drawings showing how various parts reflect light. This is similar to putting together a composite drawing. If you are going to render a chrome strip, see what one looks like in a photograph. Then, with reference to your established light source, capture the same character of reflection in your rendering. Again, the transition step from subject analysis to setting up the rendering is to do a number of value studies.

Value Studies

Value studies are used to develop the basic plan and layout for a rendering. Essentially they are quick, loose sketches in which accuracy in either perspective or technique is not important. First make a quick pencil layout of the object to be rendered. Then, using a soft graphite stick, or carpenter's pencil, boldly stroke in basic values, shadows, and reflections (figures 5-13 to 5-16). An eraser may be used to remove graphite to create a highlight or crisp up sloppy edges. Because these value studies are quick, it is easy to explore many possible layouts and lighting effects. The final rendering may be a composite of the ideas explored in the studies.

The following discussion explores the visual problems you should be solving with value studies. By dealing with these considerations before you become involved with the actual rendering, you will become more familiar with the subject and have more compositional control over the rendering.

Point of View

The object you wish to render may be manipulated on paper to find a viewing angle that best describes your interest in the object and what you want to communicate, as well as a view that seems natural for the product (figure 5-17). For example, if I designed a utility box insert for fishing tackle, I might show the box open, sitting on a dock, being viewed from a sitting position. The visual implication would be that a fisherman is looking at his tackle box open beside him. Through value studies a number of different points of view of an object can be tried until you find the best one for your rendering.

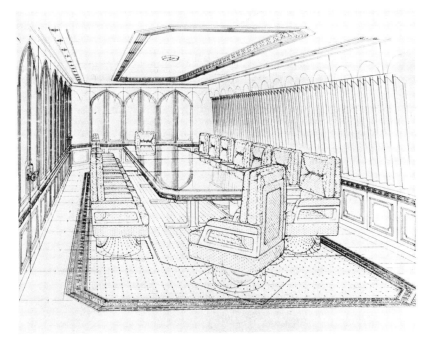

5-13. Line Drawing for Aircraft Interior, Mark Bonnette, Walter Dorwin Teague Associates. This line drawing was the basis for value studies and later renderings. The rigid stiffness of the drawing softened with value and color application.

5-14. Charcoal Value Study for Aircraft Interior, Mark Bonnette, Walter Dorwin Teague Associates. A quick graphite value study showing some possible design variations from the line drawing.

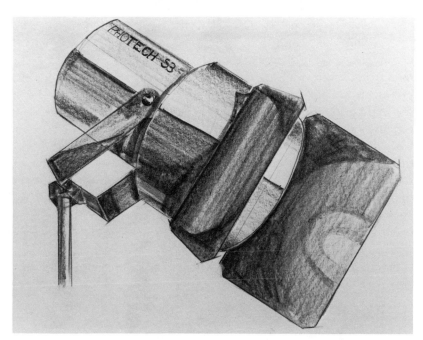

5-15. Quick (five-minute) value study for a photoflood lamp. The emphasis here is on determining the value range and desired reflections. Done with a 6B carpenter's pencil and a 6B drawing pencil.

5-16. This is the same as 5-15 but done with cool gray markers and a bold black outline.

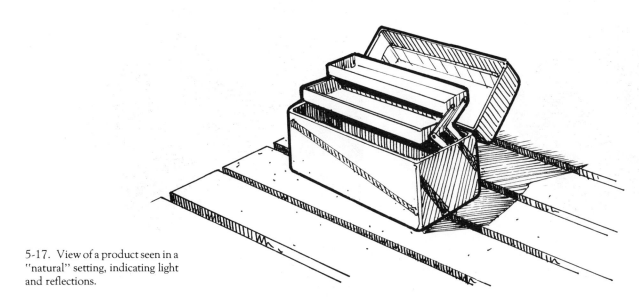

5-17. View of a product seen in a "natural" setting, indicating light and reflections.

VALUE STUDIES

Basic Light Concept

Both the basic light source and the figure/ground relationship should be determined in value studies. When determining the light source it is good to think of it conceptually, as a tool for describing the form in terms of lights and darks. Later, in the preparation of the rendering, all the highlights and shadows will be figured out. It is the basic direction of the light, the strength (brightness) of the light, and the use of shadows you are concerned with here (figures 5-18 to 5-21).

It is customary for light to strike an object from the front, off to one side; it may be thought of as coming in over either the left or right shoulder of the viewer. This way the primary surface of the product will receive the most light, and the shade side of the object and the shadow will fall back, providing a strong contrast to the light surface. This contrast helps focus the viewer's attention on the primary surface and creates a leading edge, or focal point, in the rendering. The leading edge will receive the strongest highlights in the rendering and the primary surface will be the most interesting surface on the product. (This is usually the working surface of the product—keyboard, control area, or the "front" on furniture and automobiles.) Try to avoid lighting the product from directly in front; this creates equal values on both sides of the leading edge and tends to "flatten out" the rendering rather than creating a three-dimensional effect.

Related to the light source is the value range you select for rendering the product. Remember that strong contrasts between the different surfaces of the product (one side to another) help us see it as being three-dimensional. You want to plan the drawing so that light surfaces are set off by dark areas (chiaroscuro). Therefore, with a narrow value range, such as three light grays, it will be difficult to develop strong contrast on a product.

Figure/ground relationships can be used as shortcuts to rendering.

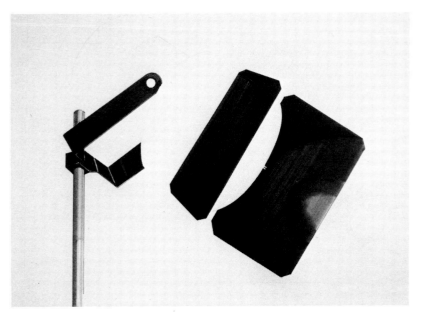

5-18. Photoflood Light, Step One. A light-line drawing has been made as a guide for the markers. Dark areas have been put in and basic reflections indicated.

5-19. Photoflood Light, Step Two. The basic values for the entire product have been put down along with shadows and vent details.

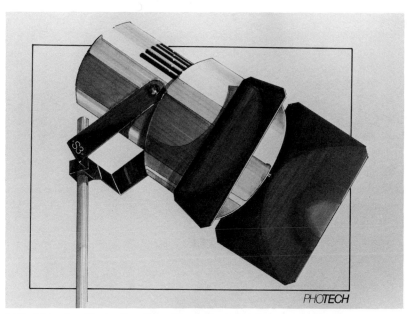

5-20. Photoflood Light, Step Three. White highlights have been painted in with opaque, and black linework has been added to make the edges crisp.

5-21. Photoflood Light, Step Four. The final graphics have been applied with transfer lettering, and a geometric line background has been added for composition.

5-22. Simple sketches showing highlights and shadows.

VALUE STUDIES

Less important parts of a product and details may be silhouetted or simply described by shadows, rather than taking the time to render them (e.g., car interiors, bottom housings on products, handles, cords, antennae, and switches). The flat, dark silhouette of a car interior indicates the dashboard, seats, steering wheel, and other interior elements, while acting as a contrast for the rendered exterior. By placing an element of the drawing against a large dark area (either a shadow, dark surface, or background) and leaving that element primarily unrendered, the silhouette will describe the form (figure 5-23).

Cast shadows lying across a part or behind it can also be used to describe the form. This technique works well for switches and edges in low relief on a surface. High-contrast photography shows this very well. In rendering, however, the contrast is not as strong (figures 5-24 to 5-26).

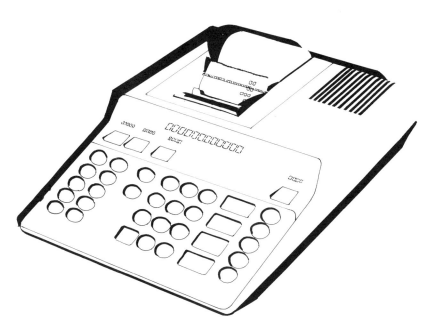

5-24. Shadows describe this form with only a minimal use of line.

5-23. Darks and negative space can be used to describe an object.

5-25. This high-contrast photo of a product demonstrates how light, shade, and shadow can describe a form without the use of linework.

Backgrounds

Backgrounds may serve three basic purposes in a rendering: to give compositional transition from the drawing to the page; to provide a suggestion of the environment in which the product typically exists; and to provide the rendering with a three-dimensional appearance. By exploring backgrounds in your value studies you can also plan for reflections on the object, achieve a better description of transparency, determine how the page will lay out, and decide on any auxiliary drawings you may need to explain the product (figure 5-27). Refer to chapter 7 for a discussion of background techniques. In the value studies you are interested in planning how the background will be used, rather than the specific rendering of it.

Special Effects

Often an accidental benefit of value studies is discovering a special effect that may make your drawing more visually memorable. Because the studies are small and the drawing tools large and more freely handled than when using them on a rendering, a gesture, stroke, or bit of color may suggest a composition, lighting effect, bold outline, or texture that would not have occurred in a more carefully drawn, larger drawing. These effects can then be planned into the final rendering. It is important to maintain the strength and gestural quality of the "special effects" found in the value studies. Try not to be overly cautious when reproducing these effects. A few broad marker strokes usually work better than outlining an area and filling it in.

Focus

Perhaps the most important use of value studies is to determine how best to show your product so that the viewer sees it from your point of view. When you design a product there are features you want to communicate to the viewer that separate it from other similar products. It is important to make these features obvious to the viewer; otherwise he will compare your design to what he sees, or knows, about other products. Generally, you want to put the most interesting and/or important part of the product and the highlights in the same area. Compose the drawing so that most of the detail and rendering occur in that area. The rest of the object and the background serve to support this focal point and may actually require very little rendering.

From the preceding discussion you can see that value studies are just sketches for designing a rendering. The remainder of this chapter deals with the specifics of rendering. You will notice when rendering that each step builds on the previous step and your attention is so absorbed in drawing and rendering that there is little time, or opportunity, to consider the design of the rendering. Hence the importance of value studies is underscored.

5-26. High-contrast photo of an interior, eliminating all linework and using the pattern of darks to show the interior.

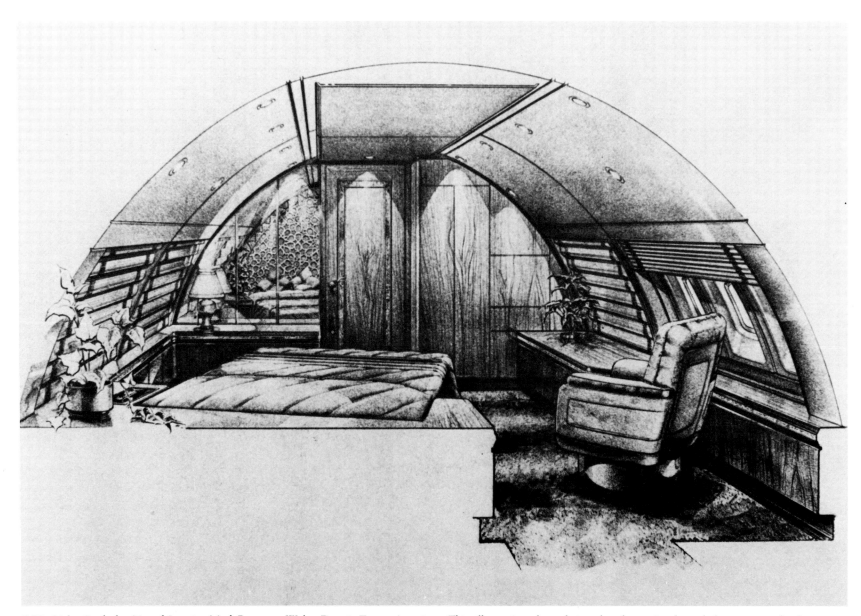

5-27. Value Study for Aircraft Interior, Mark Bonnette, Walter Dorwin Teague Associates. This silhouetting of a rendering, done by cutting through the counter and ceiling, lets us look into the environment. The light patterns cast on the walls and floor and the plants make the drawing seem real.

SETTING UP A RENDERING

Developing a Line Drawing for Rendering

After choosing the value studies from which you want to work, you need to set up a basic perspective. From this basic perspective make a series of overlays from which you can progressively build up details, organize the composition, and plan for highlights, reflections, and transparencies. This process will result in a completely detailed "light-line" drawing that you will render.

Basic Mechanical Perspective

It is not necessary to do a complete mechanical perspective of your product before rendering it. Once the basic form has been set up in perspective and landmarks have been established for the smaller elements and details, the rest of the drawing may be sketched in and tightened up with the use of a triangle and ellipse guides. The more familiar you are with perspective sketching, the freer you can be in using this technique. However, a good guideline is to spend more time with the mechanical perspective than you might consider necessary, as even small mistakes at this stage are easily compounded as the drawing progresses, and may ruin a rendering.

A common difficulty when setting up a perspective is to get the desired view of the product. A simple technique for getting a desired point of view in your mechanical perspective is to reverse the traditional procedures. Sketch out the form of your product as you want it to appear; then locate the vanishing points and the station line (usually the leading edge) relative to that sketch. Adjust the vanishing points to fit on a horizon line and move the station line slightly, if necessary, to fit a convenient perspective system. Now, ignore the sketch and draw a mechanical perspective of the basic form, putting in guidelines wherever details and graphics are to appear. For a more controlled perspective set-up, use one of the basic perspective systems. It is important to be aware of the specifics of your product's form (radii on corners, switches, small details), but you need not mechanically draw them; they may be sketched in later. When this first perspective becomes difficult to read because of all of the construction and measuring lines, make an overlay and trace only the lines you will need for your final rendering.

Perspective Overlay

Using a piece of tracing paper or layout bond over a light table, carefully transfer the important lines of the first perspective onto the fresh sheet. This should be a fineline drawing that has been tightened up with the aid of a triangle, T square, and ellipse guide. Now add a further level of detail, compose the background, and plan the page layout. There may be any number of overlays as the drawing becomes difficult to read from the sketching in of details. It is not necessary that each overlay build on the previous one. You may wish to experiment with a type of background, for example, sketching it on an overlay and disposing of it if it does not work. As you can see, this process of overlays can be a design/styling technique in addition to being a step in the rendering process. Once you have established a complete perspective drawing, it should be transferred to the rendering surface using either a light table or transfer paper. This will give you your light-line drawing.

Light-line Drawing

A light-line drawing is the drawing to which you apply the markers for the final rendering. It contains all of the perspective guidelines as well as indications for the highlights, reflections, shadows, and the like. The drawing should be made in very light pencil or chalk so that after it is rendered the lines will not show up.

Once you have transferred the perspective drawing onto the rendering surface, put in additional light contour lines to indicate reflections, highlights, and shadows. It is important to capture the character of these light effects on the surface of the product, particularly the way in which these contour lines meet with the edges of the surfaces. For example, on gloss surfaces the value areas flow into the edges; the contour lines should show this. These light lines will serve as guides for applying the markers. Once you start to put markers down it is easy to overlook a detail or generalize too much unless you have these light visual reminders sketched in.

Rendering Demonstration

The following is an outline for a basic product rendering. Each step in the outline is illustrated in the accompanying demonstrations (figures 5-28 to 5-31). Refer to the captions for specifics about each step. The outline serves as a checklist to remind you of which elements need to be considered in a rendering. Perhaps if you keep in mind that you are looking for ways to describe the light that illuminates an object rather than the lines or edges that structurally describe the object, rendering will be simpler.

I. Basic Value Systems

   Determine a light source and assign values to the major surfaces. Indicate the desired modulation of the surfaces and the areas where major reflections will be needed.

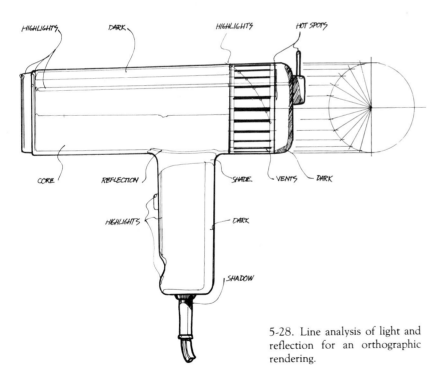

5-28. Line analysis of light and reflection for an orthographic rendering.

II. Indication of Major Highlights

   Lightly pencil in the locations of the major highlights. If possible, do not apply marker to these areas; let the white of the paper show in the rendering. The white paper is said to be the "light and life" of the rendering.
   A. Major highlights—areas where there is glare or strong reflection on a surface. Normally found on upper surfaces and edges that face the light source. These may be left unrendered (white).
   B. Minor highlights—found on small edges and on details or textured surfaces. They are put in with white opaque or white pencil after all the marker work is completed.

III. Reflections

   A glossy surface is indicated by implying a reflection from the background, showing a reflection from an unseen object in the environment, or reflecting small parts onto the surface. The more reflective the surface, the greater the contrast between lights and darks used to render that surface.
   A. Background reflections—a subtle tone of reflected color from the background is the most common. For very reflective surfaces the general shape of the background may be reflected.
   B. Environmental reflections—the two most common are horizon lines or light sources, such as a lamp or window. Other environmental reflections might be simple interior objects, table edges (for small products), buildings, and trees or foliage.
   C. Small part reflections—small parts, like switches, will reflect onto the surface on which they sit. This is the simplest form of reflection, yet probably the most important.

IV. Transparency

   The illusion of transparency is achieved by showing the collection of light and color in the edges of the transparent material, the loss of light or darkening as you look through the transparent surface, glare or major highlights on the front surface of the transparent material, and distortion of other surfaces behind the transparency.
   A. Edges—the key to the illusion of transparency. Be sure to indicate their thickness and the strength of color and highlight in them.

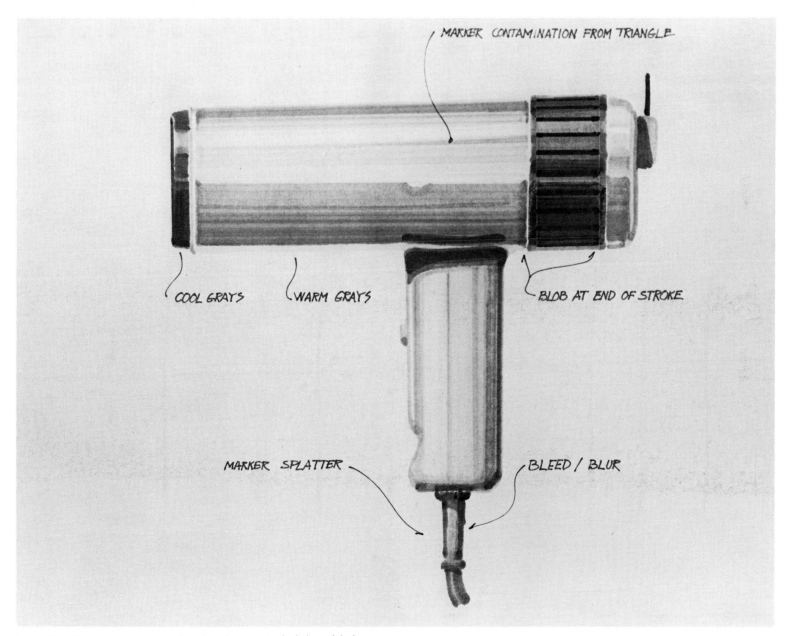

MARKER CONTAMINATION FROM TRIANGLE

COOL GRAYS   WARM GRAYS   BLOB AT END OF STROKE

MARKER SPLATTER   BLEED / BLUR

5-29. Hair Dryer, Step One. Value keys have been put in the light and dark areas. Basic marker values have been put down to "block out" the form. Some common marker problems are illustrated, such as marker splatter on the page.

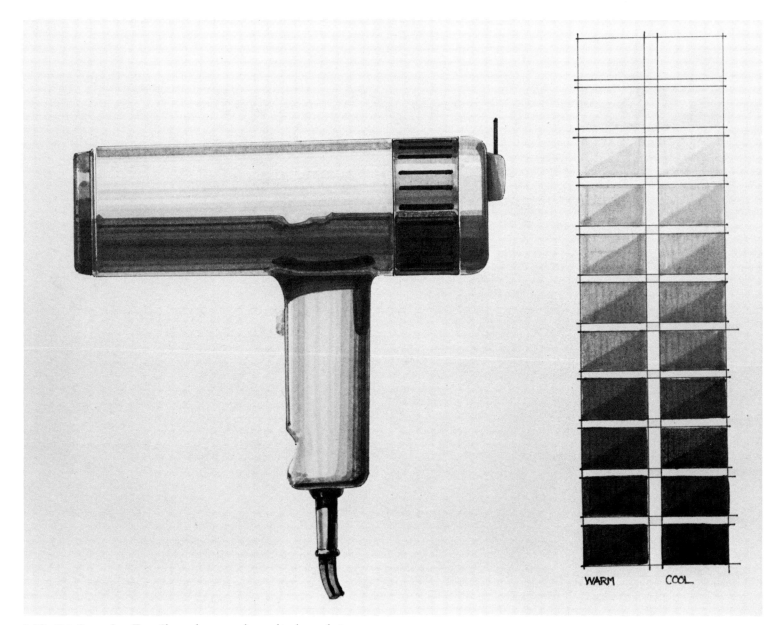

5-30. Hair Dryer, Step Two. Shows the gray scales used in the rendering—warm gray for the body and cool gray for the dark detail parts. Reflection and shadows have been put in, and shade areas have been darkened.

WARM   COOL

SETTING UP A RENDERING

B. Overlapping transparent surfaces—the dulling of colors seen through transparent surfaces aids in the illusion of volume and depth.

C. Glare—try to allow the white of the paper to show through for a strong glare. Where a softer glare is desired apply a streak of chalk when finishing the rendering.

D. Distortion—lines and edges seen through transparent material will distort slightly as they near the edges of the transparent material. Also, the lines are offset slightly when seen through a transparency. Thinking of how lines are distorted and offset when seen through water may be helpful.

V. Shadows

Shadows are put in to help separate light surfaces from each other and bring out details on a surface.

A. Major shadow areas—the shadows cast by the object itself onto the ground. These help give volume to the rendering.

B. Minor shadow areas—small parts cast shadows onto the surface of the object. These shadows help separate the details from the surface and reduce the flatness of the surface.

VI. Final Detailing

This consists of putting in some very fine lines or subtle colorwork, as well as the minor highlights. Colored pencils, chalks, and white opaque are used for most of this work.

A. Linework—fine linework can be helpful in two ways: first, to crisp up an edge and give better definition to parts; second, to add a line of color to an edge for a fine reflection or to "punch up" a highlight (make it appear brighter).

B. Color modulation—a surface of the rendered product may benefit by rubbing some colored chalk over one corner. This is usually done to warm the leading edge (by adding yellow) or cool the back edge (by adding blue) of a surface.

C. Product graphics—an important detail that can be easily overlooked. Usually a manufacturer's label or product identification is shown on a product. This graphic element needs to be indicated. Often done by carefully painting it in with opaque watercolors (designer's gouache).

D. Minor highlights—white opaque and white pencil are most commonly used to drop in minor highlights, although light tints of colored chalk are sometimes useful for putting in highlights on such things as plastics, fabrics, and other low-luster objects.

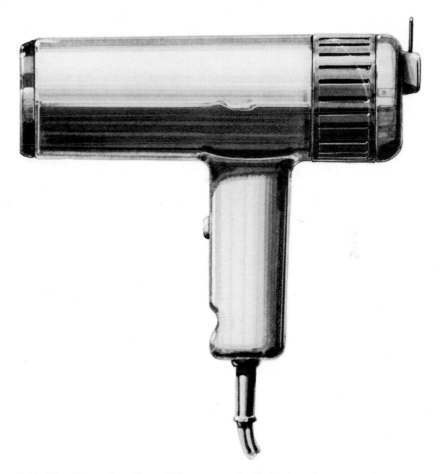

5-31. Hair Dryer, Step Three. White opaque highlights have been painted in, with some fine linework put in to define parts more clearly. You can see the halo and reflected light near the dark edges of the rendering.

CHAPTER SIX

Color in Rendering

The aim of color rendering is to offer as much richness of color as possible in order to make the rendered object believable. Reflected light, color of light, shade, and shadow all affect the local color (surface color) of an object. By indicating these elements in a rendering, the object can be seen in a believable light and atmosphere; it "exists" in three dimensions. This sense of atmosphere and believability does not require a "photo-realist" rendering—even a very stylized rendering with good visual clues allows us to imagine it as a real, possible product.

This chapter will present various uses of color in the rendering process: color sketching or color studies, full-color rendering, and limited-color rendering. A brief review of some basic color theory will make the discussion of colorwork and marker selection easier.

Color Theory

Color books abound, discussing everything from your color personality to the mixing of printing inks. If you do not have a good understanding of color, I suggest you study one of the color theory books (e.g., Munsell—see Bibliography). Here I only want to provide enough discussion of color for you to choose and blend markers, pencils, and chalks.

Colors are organized on a color wheel. (See C10 in the color section.) Three primary colors—yellow, red, and blue—are the foundation for the color wheel. All other colors are mixtures of these primary colors. Equal mixtures of two primaries create the secondary colors—orange, violet, and green. Other colors are mixtures with one of the primaries being dominant. Red orange is a mixture of yellow and red with an emphasis on red. Any two colors opposite each other are called complements; mixing complementary colors creates a neutral gray or brown.

Every color consists of three elements: hue, value, and intensity. It is important to understand these elements in order to select the appropriate color markers and make a palette of colors for rendering. A palette of colors, or markers, is the selection of markers needed to render an object. It is usually made up of a strong series of one color (such as red) and a number of modifiers and accent colors (such as violet and light orange).

Hue

A color's hue is the same as its name (e.g., red). There are many systems for naming colors, from numbers to common names. The traditional color wheel uses compound names to describe colors. For example, a range of colors from yellow to orange would be: yellow (Y), yellow yellow orange (YYO), yellow orange (YO), orange yellow orange (OYO), and orange (O). All marker brands have their own systems for naming hues, briefly described as follows (see also Appendix A):

Pantone (Letraset): Pantone coordinates markers, art papers, colored films, and printing inks by a numbering system. Each marker has a separate number; usually there is no name. The color number is the same for each product and is part of the Pantone Matching System. Theoretically, a number 109-M yellow marker will match a number 109-A film.

Design Markers: This system uses names from the color wheel (e.g., red orange) with an assigned color number, plus a number for the relative value (1 [light] to 8 [dark]). For example, a light red orange would be red orange 226-L1, and a dark red orange would be red orange 226-L8.

Mecanorma Markers: These markers have a descriptive name and number (e.g., middle red #242), but there is no association to a color wheel, and the numbers do not refer to any color order or system.

AD Markers: AD markers use common names for their colors (e.g., *New Gold*) similar to those found on paint, crayons, and so on.

Prismacolor Art Markers: This series of markers uses a sequential numbering system that orders the markers from red (number one) through orange, yellow, green, blue, violet, into a selection of "architectural" colors and "wood" colors, and ending in warm and cool grays. Each marker also has a common name (e.g., lilac).

Regardless of the naming system, you will have to select your own palette and label it. You will use a different, or modified, palette for each rendering you do. The distinctions between hues can be great, as between red and blue, or very subtle, as between red and orange. Be sensitive to this so that you can select a series of light and dark markers all of the same hue. You will find the color wheel helpful in determining hues. The color wheel is usually made with strong, bright colors.

Individual markers can be compared to the color wheel to decide which hue "family" they belong in. It may be helpful to make a color wheel with your markers to evaluate the color selection available to you.

Value

The next variable in color is value, which refers to the lightness or darkness of a hue (color). There are two value-related terms that should be noted: *tints* are light values of a hue, and *shades* are dark values of a hue. Pink is a tint of red (it has more white); burgundy is a shade of red (it has more black). The gray range in a marker system (e.g., Pantone warm or cool grays 1–11) is essentially a value range. Marker systems also offer limited value ranges for different hues (colors). Choosing a value range for a particular hue, say red, can be difficult. It is easy to mistake a different hue like red orange for a light value of red. Confusing different light hues for a tint of a hue is a common mistake. One way of guarding against this is to look for the amount of the adjacent primary color contained in the hue for which you are selecting a value range. For example, when selecting a red value range, look for the yellow content in the tints and the blue content in the shades. Do not allow the yellow or blue content to increase as the hue (red) gets lighter or darker.

Once a value range for a particular hue is selected, it is helpful to label it for future use. The simplest method of labeling is to number them 1,2,3,4,5, and so on, using 1 for the lightest value. It is helpful to indicate the brightest marker (this will be the most intense hue, as described below) of each range with a star or dot next to the number (e.g., 4*). This will help you keep your bearings when rendering, since you will choose markers relative to this intense hue, wanting one lighter or darker.

This value range will form the basis of a color palette that will be useful for future renderings. Changes in the palette will occur in the selection of accent colors. These are chosen for each new rendering situation.

Intensity

The third element in a color is its intensity. This is the degree of brilliance a color has, ranging from pure and bright to dull and grayed. This may be the most difficult element to deal with as most markers are of a strong, bright intensity, and you will often want grayed or less intense colors, particularly for rendering shadows, shade areas, and backgrounds. A good example of a low-intensity color is olive or olive drab. These colors are not particularly dark, just grayed and dull.

For each hue there is a pure, strong, intense color that can be easily identified. This will be the most intense color for that family, often called the spectrum color. Different spectrum colors have different values, yet they are all at full intensity. This is what makes the difference between value and intensity difficult. A comparison of spectrum colors to a gray scale will show this (see also figure 6-1):

Gray Scale	Spectrum Colors
White	
1	
2	Yellow
3	Yellow Orange
4	Orange
5	Red and Green
6	Blue
7	Blue Violet
8	
9	
Black	

Even with a wide selection of markers you often need a slight variation on one that is not available in a separate marker. This commonly occurs when trying to tone down a shade surface with markers that are either too bright or too dark. You want a marker slightly deeper in value and lower in intensity than the one used for a front surface. You need to vary the marker color. There are a number of ways to vary the hue, value, and intensity of your markers so that you are not stuck searching for the exact marker or using an inappropriate one.

How to Vary Hue

Layering markers, a light color under a darker one, will shift the hue of the stronger color towards the lighter one. This will also lower the intensity slightly. The application of a thin layer of pencil or chalk over

6-1. The first column shows the colors yellow, orange, green, red, blue, and blue violet. You can compare these colors to the three gray scales. The gray scales are, from left to right, AD Marker cool grays, Mecanorma cool grays, and Mecanorma warm grays.

the marker will also shift the color. Be careful not to apply it too thickly. Going over the pencil with marker again will melt the pencil into the surface and cause a better blend with the marker. This is not a good technique to try with chalk since going over the chalk with the marker will cause the marker's tip to clog.

How to Vary Value

A marker may be lightened or darkened by putting a layer of white, light gray, or black pencil over it. When working on vellum paper, gray markers may be applied to the back side to darken a color. Also, a light gray can be layered under a color to darken it.

How to Vary Intensity

A double layer of the same marker will produce a more intense color. To drop the intensity dramatically, the complementary color can be applied either in marker or pencil. In some cases a layer of marker, then a layer of white pencil with the same marker applied over it, will increase the intensity. This works best for small areas.

Choosing a Color Palette

A color palette consists of a range of markers in one hue and some accent colors. Whether you purchase markers one at a time or by the set, you will want to arrange them and label them in groups, usually organizing the three or four families of colors you use most. The accent and detail colors can be selected at the time of the rendering from your "extra" markers.

To choose markers for a palette, take a sheet of white marker paper—the kind you most frequently use—and make a test strip of all your markers. Then begin to arrange markers in hue groups and from light to dark within each group. Look for even steps (changes in value) by squinting your eyes. It will help to compare your color ranges to a gray scale. You may find some colors of the same hue and equal value, but varying in intensity, such as a light red (pink) and a dull light red (dusty rose). Normally, a range from light bright to dull dark is the most usable, so you might select the pink for the highlight areas and use the

dusty rose where a shadow falls across the light (pink) surface. A selection of four to five markers provides a good working palette. In each palette, the hue is the same, the value goes from light to dark, and the intensity moves from bright to dull.

Selecting the appropriate hue range for a product is really a matter of personal choice. The exact color match for a product will occur later in the design process and will be specified with color chips. There are some considerations that may affect which color you choose to render a product. Basic, common colors are usually the most effective as they are familiar to us and do not have negative associations for most people. Some hues to be careful with are: bluish greens (such as forest green or turquoise)—they appear cool or minty; red violets and purples are decorative and accent colors; yellow greens are also difficult since they are associated with growth rather than products.

Note: Since yellow is such a light, bright hue, it will be the most difficult to select a palette for. There are few usable low-intensity yellows since they tend to look "odd"; darker yellows often look greenish. A range from light, intense yellow to gold and light browns is about the best you can do. To this range try to add a very pale yellow for the highlight areas.

Once a good color range has been selected, accent colors are needed. These are colors that modify the range for shadows and reflections and may be used to enhance the local color of an object. These colors do not require an exact matching and are best chosen as they are needed.

Local Color

Local color is the surface color of an object. This color is modified by the amount of light falling on the object, by the color of that light, and by the direction of the light. Because of these modifications in color caused by lighting conditions you need a range of markers with which to render any particular color on an object. The usual convention is to have a highlight, middle, and shade value for each color seen on an object.

These values are usually created with the basic marker palette. Accent colors are then used to add depth and richness to the local color (figure 6-2). For instance, a shadow will have a cool blue or green cast to it, and highlight areas may have a warm yellow glow or, as with metal, a very pale, cool, blue tone.

The selection of accent colors depends upon the particular object being rendered and the lighting situation. For example, a red light on a shiny blue object will make a light violet reflection, best shown with a lilac marker or pencil. Another common use for accent colors is to define the edges of transparent materials. These edges tend to collect colors from the environment, and accent colors, being subtle and slightly "offbeat," give richness to the rendering. Some useful accent colors to complement your color palettes are lilac, yellow, magenta, purple, chrome (light) orange, olive, and mauve. The following discussion of ways in which colors can be modified will serve as a guide for selecting accent colors.

Color of Light

Direct light from the sun has a warm yellow cast to it, while indirect light from a clear sky has a cool blue cast to it. A three-dimensional object will pick up the warm glow where it faces the sun, or light source, and a cool sky tone on parts that face away from the light source. Since we are most accustomed to seeing objects in sunlight or incandescent

6-2. Truck Rendering, Dennis Huguley. This rendering also illustrates the use of accent colors. The red side shows some strong violet tints in the top front fender as well as yellow orange in the center of the truck body. The wheels show a light blue in the highlight areas to enhance the cool, metallic look.

light, this warm-to-cool accent helps us believe a rendering is three-dimensional. This warm or cool tone is a very subtle coloration that may be added toward the end of the rendering with pencil or chalk.

Reflected Light

Light that bounces off a surface picks up the color of that surface and carries, or reflects, it onto the object. A white sheet of paper next to a green wall will have a green cast to it. When rendering an object you may wish to reflect some light (color) from the ground, surrounding objects, or the background onto the object. (See C-11 in the color section.)

Amount of Light

As light is removed from an object, the object gets darker and shows less contrast; the color becomes less intense and shifts toward the brown and gray range. A bright marker color may be modified by adding the complementary color, thus making it less intense and shifting it to gray. This is particularly important in shade and shadow areas where there is little light, all of which is reflected light.

Imagination

Finally, an important consideration for modifying color is how you feel about it. A discreet use of some unusual or unexpected color can add punch or sparkle to a drawing. Photographers often do this by using a color gel on one of the lights to enhance the image. This is particularly effective when drawing on colored paper. Lines of colored pencil drawn in for definition can be a source for very effective and unusual color.

Surface Modulation

Another color consideration important in rendering is modulation across a surface. This is not a specific element of color, but rather a subtlety of light that affects the color on a flat surface. Just as volume has three basic value surfaces—a light surface, a medium surface, and a shade surface—so also will a flat surface have a three-step change in value, or a modulation, across the surface. This modulation is subtle. There is no great change in color or value, but without modulation the surface appears flat and loses some of the feeling of perspective.

If we consider a flat surface to consist of one basic color and value, modulating it would involve lightening one edge, usually the front edge, and darkening the back edge. A simple method of modulating a surface is to double-coat the back edge of the surface with marker. You may also lighten the front edge with some light pencil or chalk at the finish of the rendering.

Color Sketching (Color Studies)

Color sketching is the simplest form of color rendering. A designer may do dozens of these sketches while developing a product and working out color and details for a presentation rendering. Because these are working drawings they need to be done fast and simply. A few drawing tools are helpful along with a very limited palette of markers. These sketches are either done as orthographic views or as perspective drawings, depending upon what the designer is trying to work out. Orthographic views are ideal for exploring the proportions and layout of a product as they very accurately show the size, shape, and positions of the parts. Perspective views, on the other hand, are useful for visualizing the volumes and the overall three-dimensional form of a product. Either way the approach is the same. The following is a list of steps used in color sketching:

1. Use a light marking tool: ball-point pen, gray or black felt fineline pen, or pencil. (I caution beginners against using pencils as they tend to erase; this takes time and does not build the confidence needed to make a good line the first time.) Rough out the basic form and work out the placement of parts.
2. With the same fine line, drop in the details such as corner radii, parting lines, and graphics. Also plot highlights and shadows.
3. Select a limited palette of markers and accents (figures 6-3 and 6-4). For example, if the product is to be red, pick a range of reds, a red violet, and a yellow Prismacolor for accents. A fineline black and white opaque will be used for detailing.
4. Working from light to dark, apply the basic colors to the rough drawing, leaving the highlight areas open.
5. Apply the basic colors to those parts of the object that are different in color from the major color.

6-4. Display Sketch, Thomas A. Schutz Co. Again, an effective color sketch was built on linework and a few colors.

6-3. Display Sketch, Thomas A. Schutz Co. This sketch relies heavily on linework to show the product. A limited palette of color was used, and only a minor amount of toning or reflection was attempted.

6. Modulate the major areas with markers. Develop reflections and shade areas.
7. Clean up the drawing with dark linework. Color sketching depends heavily on linework to define areas. A useful technique for color sketching is to apply the light markers loosely and clean up the edges and tighten up the drawing with careful application of the dark values and linework. The edge of a triangle will help you to rule straight lines to crisp up edges and highlights. Add parting lines, clarify details, add vents and openings around switches. When cleaning up an edge, a vignette may be useful to block out mistakes.
8. Add white highlights with opaque and white pencil. Also add warm and cool areas with the side of a pencil point.
9. Finally, put in the typography, labels, and other graphic elements.

As you can see, there are many stages of color sketching. Almost all of these stages involve freehand work, except for the final "cleaning up" and detailing steps. To a great extent the effectiveness of the sketches depends upon the personal style and marker-handling ability of the designer.

Full-color Rendering

Just as there are many types of color sketches, there are many styles of rendering—from loose freehand work to highly mechanical, technical rendering. They are all similar, however, in that the page is fully composed and the information to be communicated is carefully considered. There are some general observations that may serve as guides as you try to develop the eye and skills needed to do renderings:

- Renderings rely less on linework than do sketches to define edges. There is greater attention to surface description to show form.
- Backgrounds usually relate to the product, e.g., the product's "natural" environment, other views of the product, a logotype, or a human figure. Backgrounds that are purely stylized decoration are few. Also, the backgrounds are incorporated into the product rendering through reflection and shadow.

- Renderings require extensive use of color. (See C12 in the color section.) A large palette is used with careful application of color and modulation of surfaces. Even in a very loose rendering you will find that casual strokes are working to suggest details.
- Detailing is important to the rendering and is usually carefully considered.
- As outlined in chapter 5, a rendering requires careful planning and considerable set-up time.

Because of the amount of work and time that goes into setting up a rendering, copies are often made of the final linework that can then be rendered, changed, or discarded as necessary. The most common method of copying a line drawing is the diazo print process. Here the final line drawing is done on vellum, and copies are run in either a blue, black, or brown line on white paper. Another method of copying is the Xerox process. Copying offers the advantage of being able to throw away mistakes without having to redraw the line copy. The original vellum drawing can be changed and new copies made without much effort.

However, copying does have its drawbacks. The greatest drawback to rendering on copies is the quality of the paper. It is usually very absorbent and may often have a coating that makes marker application difficult or frustrating. For renderings that are to be on display, or where the designer is very familiar with the form, it may be more desirable to render on marker paper or vellum as these papers are much nicer to work with and the drawings are more permanent than on copy paper.

The following step-by-step demonstration of a full-color rendering (figures 6-5 to 6-8) will give you an idea of how a rendering is developed. The captions note how some of the different drawing tools were used:

1. Set up rendering as detailed in chapter 5.
2. Block out basic color areas, working from light to dark.
3. Work at basic marker modulation of surfaces.
4. Darken shadow and shade areas to establish basic contrast.
5. Draw in details and add fine linework where needed.
6. Modulate color areas with colored pencils.
7. Paint in highlights and pencil in fine details.
8. Finish background and layout.
9. Chalk out areas for reflections and color changes.
10. Mount and cover for presentation.

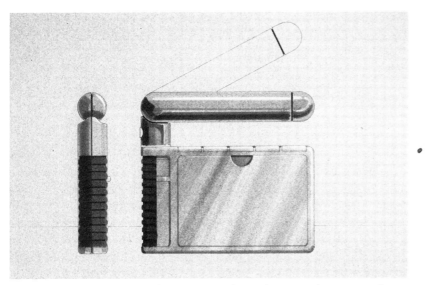

6-5. Children's Cassette Recorder, Step One. This rendering was done on gray illustration board. The first steps were to mask off the product, stroking on gray markers for the main housing, and to establish the light and dark value keys.

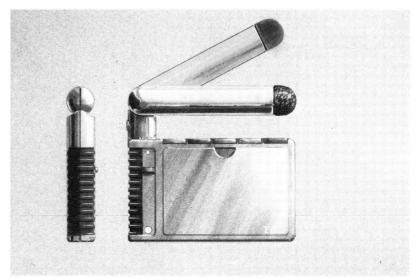

6-7. Children's Cassette Recorder, Step Three. Graphic details were added in this step as well as spot highlights. The shadows were also darkened and some final linework added to crisp up edges. Reflected light is shown at some edges with lines of colored pencil.

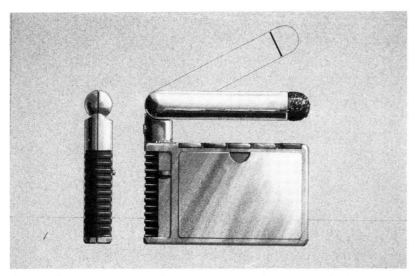

6-6. Children's Cassette Recorder, Step Two. Here the corner was highlighted, and detail color and texture were added. This work was done with chalk and colored pencils.

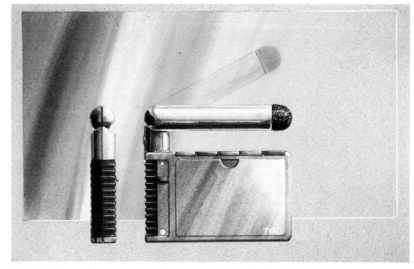

6-8. Children's Cassette Recorder, Step Four. The background was added in this step by masking over the product and stroking powdered chalk over the background area. Four colors of chalk were used to give more interest to the background. The chalk fades into the paper so as not to overpower this rather quiet rendering.

In addition to the example above, refer to the captions accompanying the other rendering examples for comments on their style and technique.

Rendering on Colored Paper

Rendering on colored paper gives a very different visual effect than working on white paper. Because the markers are transparent dyes, the paper color shows through, toning the marker color and darkening it. This means that any areas that are to be lighter than the paper color must be put in with pencil or chalk, or rendered on white paper and then cut out and pasted in place on the colored stock. The toning of the markers also means that the drawing will become more monochromatic and of lower intensity. Special care must be given to all light elements, usually those done in colored pencil or chalk, to add contrast and make the rendering pop off the page.

The basic reason for rendering on colored paper is to make quick renderings with a visual impact equal to full-color renderings. What is lost, however, is an accurate control of color and a subtlety of form, as more linework is usually employed than on white-paper renderings.

The colored papers I recommend are Canson Mi-Tientes paper, colored illustration board, or TV board. Most other colored stocks do not work well with markers, pencil, and chalk as they are too highly textured or absorbent. The paper color should be roughly the color of the object, or lighter. If you work with colored papers that are different in color from the object, or darker, more rendering and linework will be required to finish the rendering.

Utilizing the colored paper as a major color area of the rendering and darkening it for shade and shadow areas eliminate a great deal of elaborate marker application. Light areas and surface modulation are put in with colored pencil or chalk. Some colored-pencil linework for detailing and color enhancement is put in just before the final step of painting in white opaque highlights.

The toning of the markers by the colored paper gives a nice color transition between the rendering and the paper ground. The ground is no longer the lightest area, and a visual blend of ground and drawing occurs that serves to unify the page so that only a very minimal background is needed. Another nice quality of colored paper is that colored pencils and chalks seem to glow off the surface, adding a little sparkle to the rendering.

The examples shown here are all of a minimal rendering technique (figures 6-9 and 6-10 and C13 in the color section). There are more illustrative approaches that require extensive use of colored pencils over the entire surface; these are very time-consuming and do not utilize markers as a basis for the rendering.

Step-by-step Colored Paper Rendering:

1. Select a colored paper. A predominant color within the object, or a middle tone of the object color is usually best. This gives you a chance to work lighter and darker.
2. Transfer the line drawing to the colored stock using a transfer paper, colored chalk, or metallic pencil.
3. Indicate detail areas and tighten up the transfer drawing.
4. Test markers for color on scraps of the colored paper.
5. Put in your value keys—determine where the lightest and darkest values will be and leave the rest the paper color. Keep in mind that you should always be able to lighten up your lights and darken your darks later, so play it safe.
6. Do some minimal linework to define your form and details.
7. Modulate surfaces and refine details. Indicate plane changes, distances from the viewer's eye, and relationship to the light source.
8. Add darks in creases, parting lines, and vents and any detail areas of color.
9. Increase contrasts where needed to emphasize important edges.
10. Add subtle, reflected color where appropriate.
11. Add a simple background or environment.
12. Paint in and tone highlights with white opaque. Remember that all highlights are not equal in size or intensity.

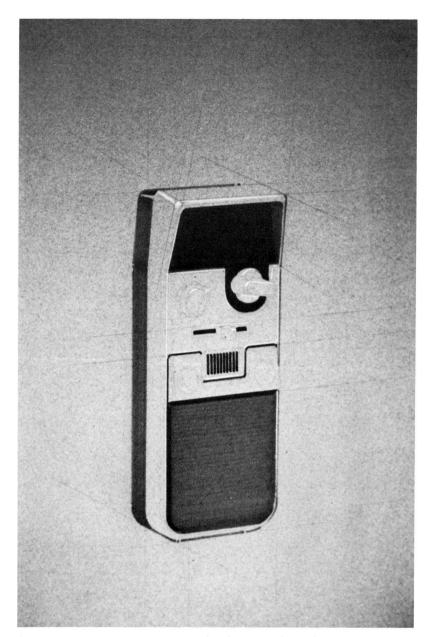

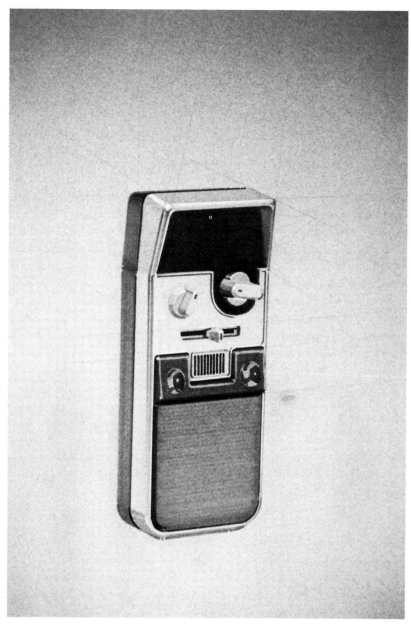

6-9. C.B., George Tiston, Step One. Colored paper rendering done on canson paper. The value keys were put down with marker, describing the basic form and leaving the colored paper to determine the middle value.

6-10. C.B., George Tiston, Step Two. Major details were rendered using marker and some colored pencil. Major color areas were established and some shading was put in.

One common problem you may want to be aware of when doing any color rendering is that after the basic color areas are put in there is often a loss of confidence. Little can be done about this other than pressing on and detailing the rendering.

Developing a talent for rendering usually requires building the necessary skills while at the same time learning to see and know what to put down. Skill development progresses from line drawing through color sketching. Renderings may first be seen as highly refined sketches. As one becomes sensitive to color and the dynamics of composition, renderings become easier and take on more vitality and personal style.

Backgrounds

Backgrounds are important compositional elements in a rendering. Their content and style are as varied as the products rendered, but there are elements common to all backgrounds since they all serve a similar purpose.

The primary function of a background is as a compositional tool, setting up the rendering so it pops off the page. The transition from the flat, white, two-dimensional page to the three-dimensional effect of the rendering is what gives the product a ground and a believable setting. Without a background the rendered products tend to float in a vacuum or look like a hole in a doughnut of white paper.

By incorporating common elements from the paper and from the drawing into the background, a successful transition can be made. Then, by further composing the background around the object, it can be dramatically set off the page.

There are some basic compositional principles that will make planning a background much easier:

- The simple geometry of the paper can be reflected in the background (figures 7-1 and 7-2). By varying it from a plain, flat rectangle with the use of color and modification of shape or texture, you combine elements of the rendered product and the paper into one transitional element.

- The natural setting, or environment, of a product can be stylized and drawn in an abstract manner which, by its simplicity, will serve as a middle ground between the object and paper (figure 7-3).

- A background may be rendered to fade progressively as it moves toward the edges of the paper (figure 7-4), thus becoming the paper.

- The object itself may have areas of unrendered paper that will link it to the paper. Repeating this in the background helps the transition between object and paper.

- Marker strokes may be used to make a simple patterned background that will serve as a backdrop behind the rendered object.

There are also some basic background principles that can be used to make the rendering seem more dramatic:

- Position the background behind the object so that as the eye moves over the object it is drawn back into the background and then onto the page.

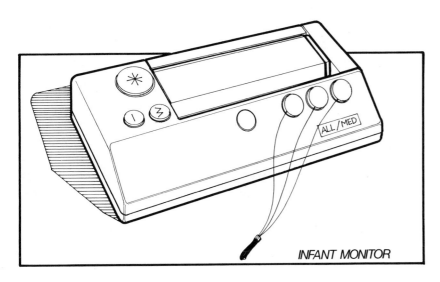

7-1. The simple rectangular background acts as a ground for the product and relates to the shape of the paper.

7-3. The addition of someone using the product provides a very stong background.

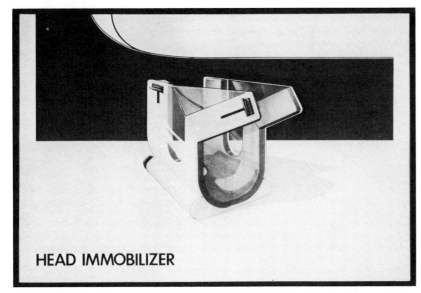

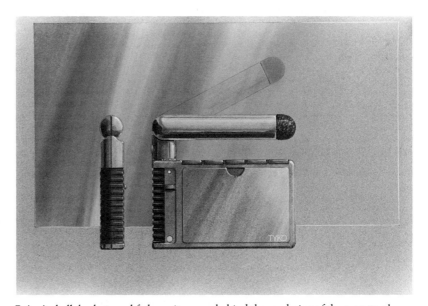

7-2. Head Immobilizer, Jim Haager. A sweep in the otherwise solid rectangular background gives a little life to this composition. A light shadow also helps hold the product to the page. Notice how the background is used to enhance the feeling of transparency in the plastic plates by reflecting the sweep onto the plastic.

7-4. A chalk background fades as it moves behind the rendering of the cassette player. The microphone is shown lightly in the background to indicate its adjustability.

- Use a more subdued color for the background than that used for the rendered object. Often a complementary color can be used effectively to set off the object by contrast.
- Do not evenly surround the object by the background (figure 7-5). Allow a simple progression of small, medium, and large proportions of the background to border the product.
- Let the leading edge move off the background and out toward the viewer.
- When using an abstract or geometric background, indicate a table line where the implied surface on which the object sits changes to a vertical back surface.
- Reflect some element of the background onto the product through color, shape, and the like (figure 7-6).

- Consider using related elements as a background. Similar products, other views of the product, or accessories that may go with the product all help the viewer understand it better.

Aside from being a transition or a way of setting up a rendering, backgrounds can also help clean up rough edges and define contours. By putting down a strong, dark contour, you can cover any loose or sloppy-edged lines or cut into the rendering to show a small contour detail. For example, you can round off the outside corners of a product by letting the background curve over the corners. This is particularly useful for cleaning up rough sketches.

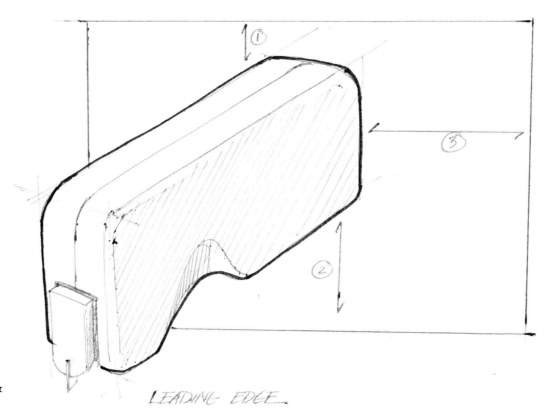

LEADING EDGE

7-5. Position the background so that the object is not centered on it.

COOL REFLECTION

WARM REFLECTION

7-6. A bright background was covered over with black to tone it down. Some areas of color were left showing and were then reflected onto the object. The cool colors are reflected on the dark side, and the warm colors are reflected on the highlight side.

Types of Backgrounds

With these basic principles in mind, consider the following examples of different types of backgrounds. The styles may be interchanged for a wide variety of possibilities.

Vignettes

This is the simplest type of background. Basically it is a dark line or group of lines that outlines a part of the object and is strongest at the back (figure 7-7).

Geometric

The most common background is a simple rectangle, often with rounded edges. There are many variations on this, such as a rectangle that fades out on one side or has an overall texture. Other geometric shapes may also be used. Three-quarter circles are effective. As the background shape becomes complicated it becomes less effective and attracts too much attention.

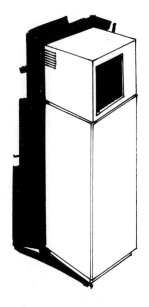

7-7. A loose, dark vignette can serve as a casual background.

Shadows

The shadow of the product forms a very natural background. It may be filled in as a gray mass or silhouetted for a light, minimal look.

Environments

Environments may be very elaborate renderings themselves or simple linework to suggest a setting (figure 7-8). For outdoor environments it is customary to suggest a stagelike shallowness by showing a tree-line and a simple ground. Objects shown in indoor environments may be accompanied by a figure or hand using the product or a surface upon which the product sits.

Typography

Renderings often include a company name, a logotype, or a symbol that is associated with a product (figure 7-9). With careful copying and rendering these elements make striking backgrounds. They are also easy to reflect onto shiny surfaces of the rendered product if desired. The relationship of typography to the product is both visual (curves, use of marker, and so on) and conceptual (identification). Typographical elements relate to the paper through the basic geometry of the letters and word or symbol forms, the white space inside the forms that is needed to read the letters, and the flat nature of letters and symbols.

Abstractions

This is a catch-all category for a wide variety of backgrounds. They are usually gestural fields of color or line. Because of the loose application style, these backgrounds are often made separately from the rendering. The rendering is then cut and glued in on top of them. This also permits the rendering to be done on white paper and then mounted on colored stock or another more decorative board.

Orthographic Views

One very useful background is made with an orthographic view of the rendered object, with basic dimensioning included (figure 7-10). The orthographic view is positioned behind the object as a geometric background would be. To strengthen this flat view of the object, an exaggerated selection of line weights may be used, often done in a dark color (brown, blue, or rust, for instance) rather than black. Also, the ortho-

graphic view may require that a flat value, or series of values, be laid down over it to give it the necessary body to hold the product rendering in place.

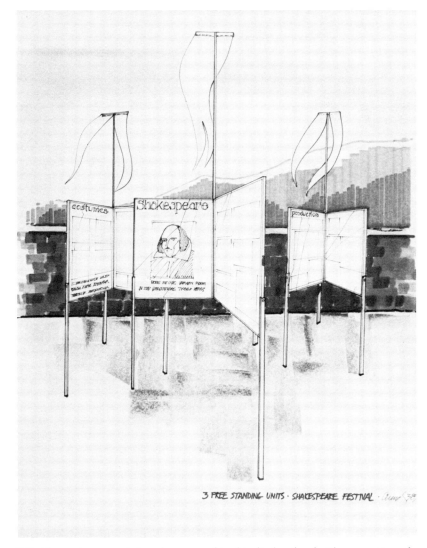

7-8. The environment is loosely suggested in this display sketch. The suggestion of a ground, wall, and tree line are all dark to provide a strong contrast to the light treatment of the display panels.

7-9. The name of the product that is used as a background for the car rendering was made by cutting a stencil of the letters and rubbing chalk over the stencil. Later a fineline border was drawn around the letters.

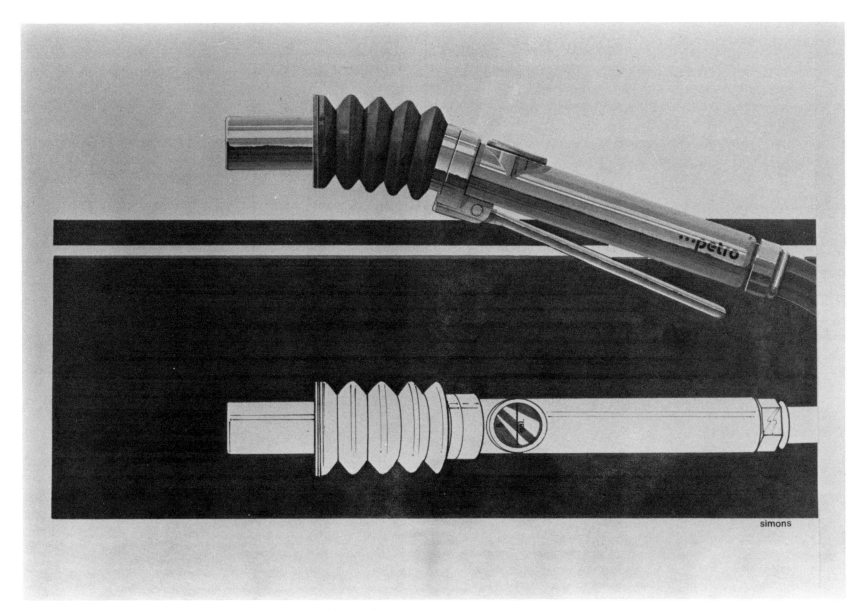

7-10. Gas Pump, George Simons. An orthographic top view of this gasoline pump
serves as the main background element. The rendering was done in full color, which was
set off well by the dark silhouette and the linework of the background.

Background Techniques

Below are some simple techniques for making backgrounds that are based upon the materials used. They involve either a careful, direct application of markers and chalk, or a masking and cutting procedure that takes more planning but allows for freer use of materials.

Marker Backgrounds

The markers are handled in the same manner for a background as they are in a rendering. However, they are applied as flat, two-dimensional color and often with a straightedge to get a crisp, mechanical field that contrasts with the contours of the rendered product. First, the background is lightly penciled in, then the edge line of the product is defined with the background color, and the rest of the area is filled in with vertical strokes. At least three colors of marker should be used, ranging from a dark to a light. The background area closest to the leading edge of the rendered product should be predominantly light and get darker as it moves away from the product. This adds a richness to the color and depth to the rendering (figure 7-11).

Flo-master Backgrounds

Using Flo-master inks requires extensive masking as the ink is applied with a cotton pad. Color may be built up layer upon layer and a rich, free field bound by a clean edge is produced. It is common to put down a very bright, vibrant color and then cover it with a darker color, leaving only "splinters" of the brighter color showing.

Chalk Backgrounds

Chalk may be used like the Flo-master inks, using a solvent such as rubber cement thinner or lighter fluid. To do this, powder the chalk on a tray. Then, with a cotton pad wet with solvent, pick up some chalk. The solvent will melt the chalk and it can be "painted" on by smearing the pad over the background area. Again, careful masking is required. A direct use of chalk can be made either by rubbing the dry powder into the background or by using the chalk stick in the background. When using chalk, as with all media, be sure to use at least three colors for depth and richness. An advantage to the direct use of chalk is that it can be erased if a mistake is made or if edges need to be cleaned up.

Typographic Elements and Linework

Another consideration in organizing the rendered page is the layout and application of any verbal information or identification. This is important whether the rendering is freestanding, part of a series of renderings, or a plate in a formal storyboard presentation. The layout and handling of all the visual elements of the page contribute to the important first impression the client (or whoever) has of the presentation. There is a good chance that, if the presentation does not seem clean and professional, a negative reaction may prompt the client to look for problems and to be wary of the design rather than being open and anticipating a successful presentation.

There are two major elements to be dealt with when laying out a page: typography and linework.

7-11. Markers can be used to stroke in a single backround. Here the markers were also stroked over the shape of the stapler, which was later defined by linework and detailing.

Typography

Typography refers to the verbal information on a rendering; it should be kept to a minimum. You want the viewer to read the drawing rather than a description of the product. Also, in order to be read from a distance, the type would have to be large or bold, which would detract from the drawing; moreover, it is time-consuming to put down. Some type is always needed, however. It may be simply the identification of the design firm or support information for the drawing. The information is usually a headline that tells what the product is, which drawing it is (i.e., A,B,C or 1,2,3) or the project name. There may be secondary information such as a listing of important features, a brief description of the function of the product, or labeling of parts and materials. Finally, some identification of the drawing and project may be desired. As with a technical drawing, the date, designer, project, page, and so forth may be recorded.

Where this information is located will depend on the drawing. However, it should be kept simple, readable, and to a minimum. The following suggestions may help guide your use of written information:

- Three letter sizes (point sizes) can be used, one for each class of information: large (e.g., 72 pt.) for headlines and identification numbers, moderate (e.g., 24 pt.) for features and detail information to be read as the drawing is viewed, and small (e.g., 16 pt.) for information of record.

- The office label, or business card, is often applied to the lower right corner as a simple form of identification.

- As much as possible, keep the typography away from the drawing and toward the edges of the paper. Leave a good margin, however, so that the type does not fall off the paper. Also, establish common margins for the type. If the heading is flush left, an accompanying listing of details should also be flush left, all with a common margin. Horizontal lines can also be established so that type on one side of a rendering will line up with type on the other side.

- Information usually reads from the upper left to the lower right corner. Organize the information to flow in that direction.

- It is far easier to read uppercase and lowercase letters than all uppercase. When putting down more than one or two words, avoid exclusive use of uppercase letters.

- Do not mix styles of typography. You may use a bold or italic face, but keep to one font.

- Avoid decorative typography. Nonexaggerated typefaces are the most legible. Note: to check quickly for basic legibility of a type face, check the uppercase H, O, and A. They should have an outline of a square, circle, and triangle, respectively. The more they are modified from these basic shapes, the less legible the type will be. A stylized type will tend toward one basic shape, such as a square.

- Use tight letter-spacing for composition and legibility. There are two basic ways to apply type: by hand or using transfer letters. For large headlines, transfer lettering is recommended as it is difficult to draw large letters without spending a good deal of time. For smaller sizes, either hand-lettering or transfer letters are fine. When doing basic hand-lettering there are some simple guides to keep in mind:

1. Draw a series of parallel lines the height of the letter you want. Use the x height as a guide if using upper- and lowercase letters. (The x height is the size of a lowercase x, which is the visual size of a line of type.) (figure 7-12.)

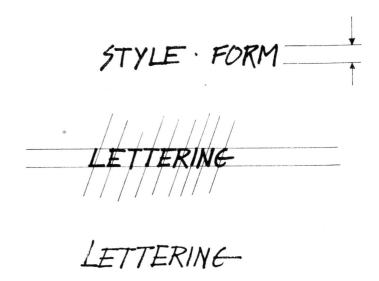

7-12. These three examples show the x-height of lettering, the slant, and a freehand style.

2. Keep a consistent cant, or slant, to the letters. A line drawn through vertical height will show the slant.
3. The gesture of the basic strokes should be consistent. There are six basic strokes used to make all letters: vertical, horizontal, forward and backward slants, and forward and backward curves (figure 7-13). Practice them separately and in combination.
4. The line weight of the letters should be controlled and not too thin. Do not use a chisel point if you are not too comfortable doing calligraphy.
5. Try to develop a style to your lettering that has some character and is consistent.

I─/\◯

BASIC STROKES · SLANTED

CASUAL LETTERING

EXAGURATED LETTERING

7-13. The six basic strokes—vertical, horizontal, forward and backward slants, forward and backward curves.

Linework

In addition to typography, some linework may be used to help organize the page. Again the best advice is to keep it simple and to a minimum. Horizontal and vertical lines are generally all that is needed. Occasionally a diagonal may add to the typography, but it should not go behind the rendering as it conflicts with the eye movement. A simple horizontal line at the bottom of the page is often sufficient. This establishes a ground for the typography and implies the margin. Often a fine margin line is drawn an inch or so in from the edge. Beyond this, additional lines are unnecessary. Keeping lines simple and light is a good rule. They should be used only to help organize the layout and not for decorative purposes. If you feel there is a need for more lines, there is probably something wrong with your background or placement of the rendering, and more lines will not help.

Coordination and Consistency

A final consideration when laying out the page is how it is to coordinate with other presentation sheets or storyboards. Consistency from board to board is also important. The viewer need not reorient for each new board and can pick up the new information easily and quickly when a similar and consistent format is used.

The basics for consistency are obvious: same size or coordinated boards, same use of typography and linework, and comfortable styles of drawing. It is important that one board does not overpower the other boards. Try to achieve a similar visual impact from board to board, depending upon the importance of the information. You may find that a technical drawing or detail drawing has to be beefed up with color, line weight, or size in order to hold up visually to a rendering. A simple unifying element may be added to a series of boards to hold them together. Often a stripe across the edge or an information block in the corner is all that is needed for more casual presentations. As the presentation becomes more formal, all the variable elements—typography, linework, background, layout, and page size—will be coordinated in style and laid out on a grid for consistency.

Specialized Rendering Techniques

This chapter explores some rendering techniques that have more limited applications than straight marker rendering or are specific variations on marker techniques. These new techniques may be used strictly as presented or, more likely, you will begin to combine these techniques to find a comfortable, personal working style.

Regardless of the materials or style used to produce a rendering, the groundwork is always the same. It is good to remember that a rendering describes the light about an object. It is the relative value, contrast, and the location of highlights, shadows, and color that are important in rendering. With each of the techniques described here it is assumed that an accurate line drawing of the product has been made, that a light source has been established, and that highlights and shadows have been planned. This is the basic information needed to make any rendering.

The techniques described in this chapter offer a choice of a wide variety of materials. However, each technique is based on a specific use of material, and the final rendering relies on the visual qualities of that material, or the style of its application, for its impact. These techniques are adhesive color film rendering, tape drawing, dissolved chalk, dry chalk, and vellum rendering. They are presented for their value as quick rendering techniques and their impressive visual qualities. They each have drawbacks that limit their use. You may find that letting the nature of the product determine the rendering technique used is far less frustrating than trying to render everything with a favorite technique or "house style." For example, a dissolved chalk rendering works best for orthographic views of products done on a large paper size such as 18" x 24."

Adhesive Transparent Colored Films

Using adhesive transparent colored films for rendering produces a bold, colorful drawing. Because the films put down flat color, and bold, dark outlines are needed to conceal the cut lines, films are best used in diagram-type line drawings and in drawings in which elaborate detailing or subtle form development is not needed. (See C14 and C15 in the color section.)

Transparent colored films come in a wide range of colors and patterns and may be bought in a glossy or matte finish. These films come in sheet form with a backing sheet to protect the adhesive. They also are available in a range of percentage color tints. For example, a 100 percent blue will be a solid color, and a 10 percent blue will have only one-tenth of the color. Thus, it will be a very light, pale blue. Since the films are transparent, overlapping them causes a darkening and mixing of the color. A 20 percent blue over a 10 percent blue will create a 30 percent blue. Yellow over blue creates a green. Because the adhesive on the film is light it may be repositioned, or picked up and layed down again, as desired. When the final positioning has been made, the film should be burnished (rubbed) down with a broad tool to make the strongest bond with the paper.

The basic procedure for using these films is as follows: first, lay the sheet over the area to be covered with the film, cut an oversized piece, and peel it off the backing sheet. Be sure to use a sharp blade to cut the film and use a light touch so as not to cut through the backing sheet. You will notice that the backing sheet is heavier and has more fiber than the film, making it more difficult to cut. Now, position the film on the drawing, overlapping all around the area to be covered. Lightly burnish the film down and trim off the overlap with a sharp blade.

Rendering with Films

The preparation needed for film rendering is a good line drawing of the product and a palette of films. The palette should have at least three films for each color to be used—a very light tint (10 to 20 percent), a moderate tint (30 to 50 percent), and a full color (80 to 100 percent). The basic procedure is as follows:

1. Make a line drawing of the product on a heavy paper or board; three-ply bristol board is good. This is done to avoid cutting through the paper as the film is cut.
2. Ink (with a permanent ink) the line drawing. Remember to use three line weights and leave highlight edges alone. It is difficult to add linework after the film has been applied. These lines also serve as guides on which to cut the film and hide the cut lines.
3. Very lightly, pencil in the highlight areas on the line drawing. You will want to leave these areas white.
4. Use the above-mentioned procedure for cutting and positioning the films. Start with the largest, lightest areas to be covered first and work toward the darker, smaller areas. There are two reasons for

this: the layering of film darkens the color, and large films over smaller pieces can cause problems by trapping air under the film at the edges of the small pieces.
5. When a large sheet of light film is put down, cut the edges near the highlight with a sharp knife and a straightedge. Cut edges should be crisp and mechanical so that there is a look consistent with the line drawing and the even, crisp look of the film surface.
6. Utilize the buildup of color and apply additional films over the light ones to get a deepening of color. Leave a thin edge of the lightest tint showing around the highlights.
7. If air bubbles appear under the film, try to burnish them out, working from the center to the edges. A small pinhole in the film will eliminate air bubbles that persist.
8. Film rendering requires very little detailing. Small highlights may be cut in at the end, and spot highlights may be painted in with white opaque.

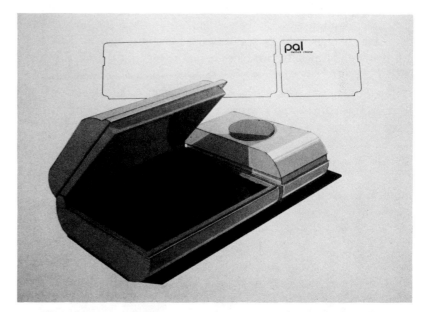

8-1. Ultrasonic Denture Cleaner, Al Ransenberg. A further use of colored films is shown here by the indication of shadows and water. This is more of a rendering approach to using films than a diagram approach. The rendering still has the crisp, bold, direct look of a diagram, however.

As you can see by the accompanying examples, film rendering has a very nice appearance with a crisp, diagramlike style. There are pattern films you may wish to use to get more decorative graphic effects. The most common of these films are dot and line patterns. One note about using film is that it does not work well visually with other media such as markers or pencils. Because of the mechanical nature of the films, they appear to work best with other mechanical-type lines and materials, such as tapes, Rapidograph pens, and transfer lettering. By using the colored films to indicate shadows and transparency (e.g., the water in figure 8-1), a film rendering will look less like a diagram and more like a very crisp, bold marker rendering.

Tape Drawings

Tape drawings are full-scale, orthographic line drawings of large objects. The drawings are executed with black, flexible (crepe) tape and are often rendered with dyes, chalk, or an airbrush. Tape drawings are used extensively in automotive design, where the technique has been refined to a high level of sophistication, producing very handsome full-scale renderings. In product design the technique is usually more basic and is used to rough out elevations for quick scale and proportion evaluation. Supermarket check-out stands, chairs, outdoor street furniture, exhibit panels, and exercise machines are examples of products that lend themselves to tape drawing.

Rendering with Tape

There are three phases to tape drawing: preparation of the surface, application of the tape, and rendering (if desired). The first phase is important as you need an unusual working surface. It should be a rigid, smooth, vertical surface that stands flush on the floor and will accept pins and staples. A large bulletin board or an inexpensive sheet of Celetex (4′ x 8′) from a lumberyard will work nicely. On this surface a sheet of drawing paper is stretched; Clearprint tracing paper with a ¼-inch grid works well. To stretch the Clearprint, staple one end of the roll to the end of your board, unroll the paper to the desired length, pull it tight, and staple the other end. Do not spare the staples and be sure to tack down along the top and bottom edge of the paper as well.

With the surface thus prepared, you are ready to put the tape down. In some cases you may already have a full-scale orthographic drawing of a product that you wish to make into a tape drawing or to modify as a tape drawing. This orthographic can be stapled up under the Clearprint as an underlay to work from.

Drawing with tape offers some strong advantages when used on a large scale. Tape comes in many widths, so various line weights are readily available. Tape goes down fast: a 12-foot, ¼-inch line takes only seconds, and it is repositionable for experimenting and correcting mistakes. Crepe tape also tends to lay down in straight lines, yet it will produce regular curves very easily. Naturally, as with any medium, some experience is necessary to handle it comfortably. There are a few general tips that may help:

1. Stick the end of the tape to the paper. Then unroll the tape with one hand and tap it to the surface (pat it down) with the other. After it is lightly tapped into place, go back and lightly rub it down for a more secure hold. Try not to pull or stretch the tape too much as it may "shrink" back after it is put down, gapping and wrinkling the paper.
2. Extend the hand that holds the tape in the direction of the line. Use this hand to control the direction of the tape line. For curves, slowly arc the tape hand as you pat the curve down.
3. Hold a cutting blade in the patting hand to cut the tape from the roll at the end of a line. It is frustrating to search for a blade at this point, so keep one in hand. An alternative to this is to keep a slightly long thumbnail filed flat to tear the tape against. Pinch the tape to the board with the thumbnail and pull the roll up against the thumb; the tape will rip.
4. You may feel tape drawing is like wallpapering—a one-and-a-half-person job—the constant measuring and checking of lines being a nuisance. To avoid this, try to measure most of the landmarks at one time and work from the grid in the paper. Also, pin a working orthographic sketch to the wall for reference.
5. Keep a wide variety of tape sizes handy. While most of the linework will be done with thin tape, there are many parts and lines that can be graphically done as solid blacks and heavy lines.

The accompanying examples (figures 8-2 to 8-8) may give you the best idea of how to do a tape drawing. I find there is no one best procedure; let the product dictate the approach. Generally, a ground line should be established. A bold, black, two-inch tape line along the base of the paper is visually strong and "holds the drawing down." From here the basic outline of the product is laid down. It helps to establish a light source and use a thin tape (⅛ inch or ¼ inch) on surfaces that face the light and a slightly thicker one (¼ inch or ⅜ inch) for surfaces in shade or shadow. With the basic shape down, major dark areas and parting lines can be put in. These serve as landmarks for judging proportions, as well as giving the drawing some boldness so that we begin to see the design as a product. When putting in small parts and details you may find occasion to use a black marker for a tight radius or detail that is awkward to do in tape. Markers are also nice for adding graphics for a finished look. Once the tape work is done the drawing may be used as is or rendered.

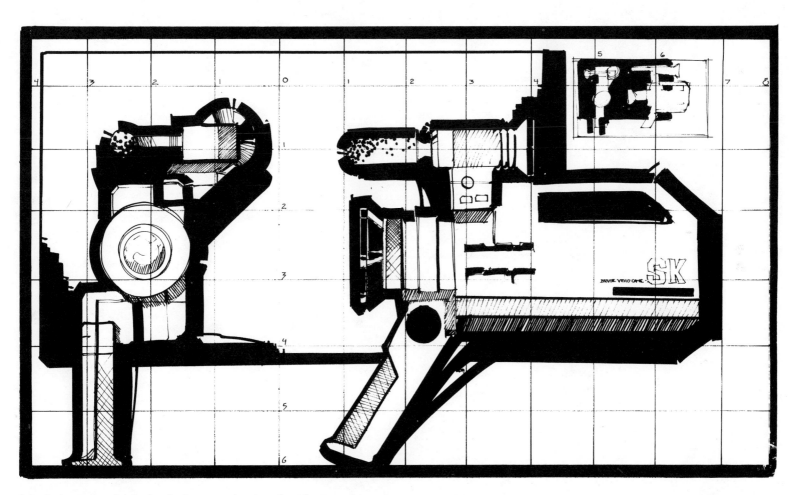

8-2. Orthographic sketch plan for large tape drawing of a video camera.

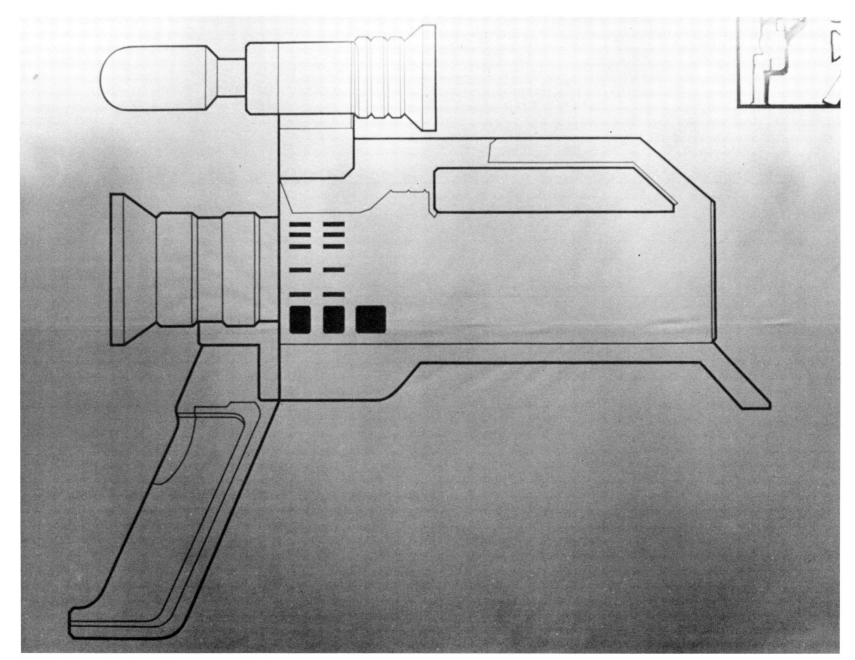

8-3. Tape linework for large video camera tape drawing.

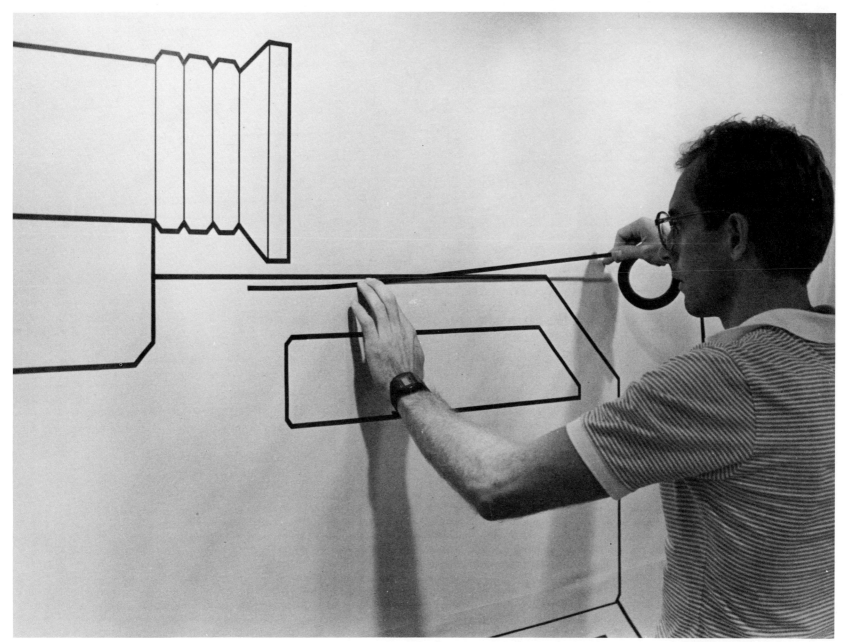

8-4. Flexible black tape (¼ inch) was used to "draw" lines for this tape drawing of a video camera. Holding the tape out with one hand and patting it down with the other gives enough control to "draw" either straight or curved lines.

TAPE DRAWINGS

143

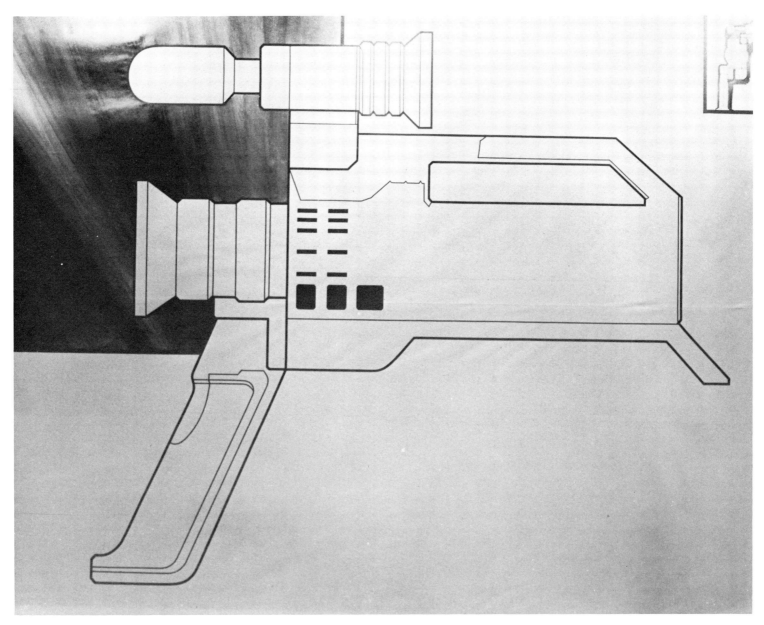

8-5. A background was added to the completed tape drawing. The background was put in by masking the video camera and stroking in liquid dye with a cotton pad.

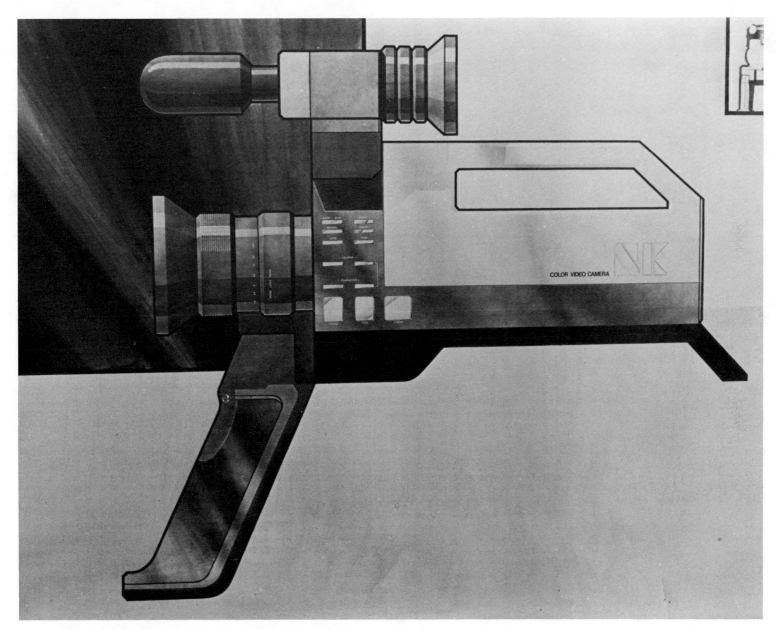

8-6. Completed Tape Drawing of a Video Camera, Brian Kolbus and George Simons (approximately 8 feet high). The rendering of the camera was done primarily with an airbrush, using paper masks to avoid overspraying.

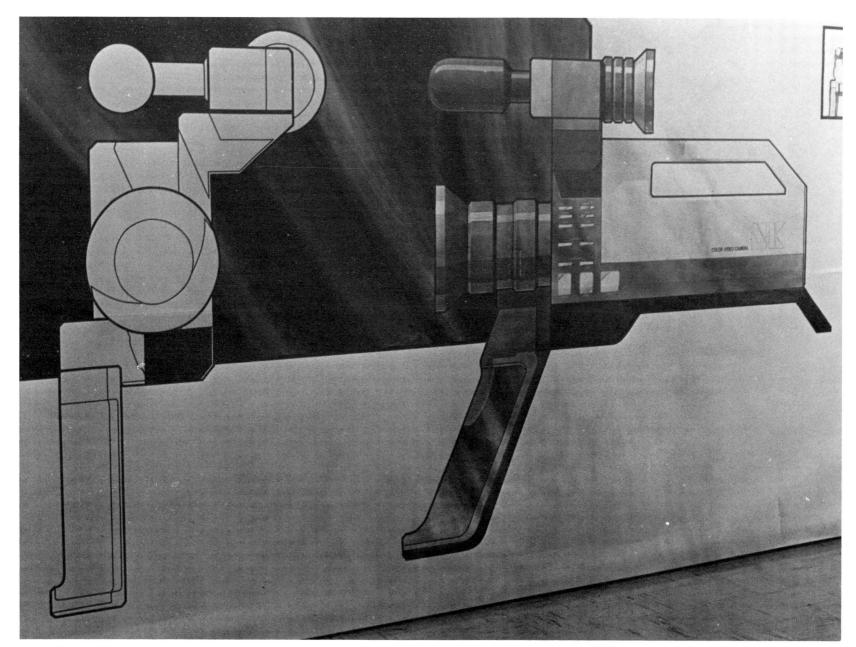

8-7. Full view of the tape drawing showing an unrendered front view and a rendered side view.

Rendering a tape drawing can be a fairly time-consuming and expensive task of masking and airbrush work or a quick process with minimal masking using chalks, markers, and spray dyes. The descriptions and examples here were all done as quick studies for further product development.

Most products have a basic shape and color. Boldly putting these in and adding a background is often enough to carry the tape rendering without elaborate rendering of details. One reason for this is the strength and boldness of the tape linework. Also, the scale of the drawing may be impressive enough to override the need for elaborate rendering of details.

Keeping in mind the light source, fill in the major color area. Try to use more than one color for this, moving from the light side with a warm tone to the shade side with a cool tone. You will probably want to mask off parts of the drawing when applying color. This can be easily done using tracing paper with tape lapping over one edge. Lay the tracing paper in place, using the tape to hold it and serve as the edge of the mask. Another technique is to stretch a sheet of tracing paper or Clearprint over the entire tape drawing and cut out the areas where you wish to apply the color. Be careful not to cut through the Clearprint surface of the drawing. Cut on top of the tape lines whenever possible. Once major color areas are put down, small color areas can be put in. For some of them, hand-held masks, or dodges, can be used to protect areas of the drawing from color. The most common of these is a piece of paper cut to the desired shape and held in place while the color is applied. This often results in messy hands, but it is quick and effective.

As color is applied more elaborately, you may want to remove some of the tape. Obviously, tape can be removed where a strong color will define an edge. The tape can also be removed to leave a white line within a color area. This is effective for creating a white line between the product and a dark background or for highlight edges. To get a thin highlight edge along a dark parting line, pick the black tape up and shift it 1/16 inch. This will leave a fine white line running along the black tape line. A spot highlight on that line may be added by cutting a small scoop out of the black tape.

Tape drawings are impressive but have a short life. They may be rolled up for storage, but the tape will soon fall off. Like mockups, they are good development tools and effective support drawings in a presentation.

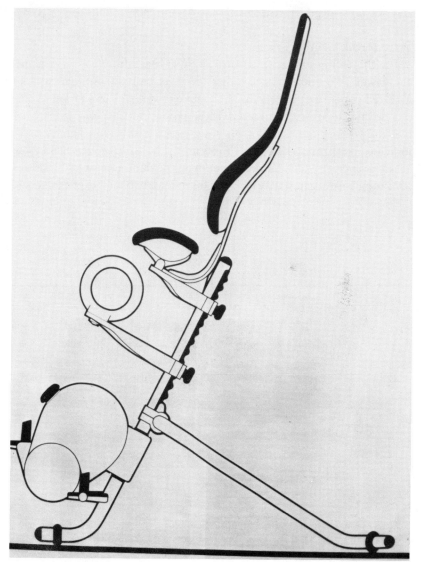

8-8. Full-scale Tape Drawing of an Exercise Chair, David Skinner (approximately 7 feet high). This tape drawing was not intended to be rendered. The lines are very bold, and solid black areas were put in to define parts.

Chalk Renderings

There are three basic ways to use chalk in rendering: as a stick, as powder, and dissolved on a cotton pad with a solvent. The use of chalk in stick form is more of a sketching technique or a detailing tool. The other two methods of using chalk will serve to illustrate its capabilities and perhaps suggest further uses.

Powdered Chalk Wash

For this technique a soft, absorbent paper that takes both marker and chalk well is required. Papers that bleed excessively are undesirable. Colored papers can also be used effectively with this technique.

The first steps are the same as with all rendering: develop a fine pencil line drawing of the product on your paper, establish a light source, indicate highlights, and, very importantly here, indicate all shadow areas. Using very dark markers, put in all the dark areas and dark lines for the entire drawing (figure 8-9). This includes shadows, parting lines,

dark or shade areas—everything. With this basic marker work done the chalk may be applied.

Take your chalk sticks and powder them by rubbing the edge of a blade against the stick. For each color desired in the rendering, make a light, medium, and dark powder. Also, make some white, yellow, and violet powder. Before applying the chalk, a frisket paper can be fitted and cut around the body of the object to mask off large areas where chalk is not wanted. Using a soft cotton pad, pick up some of the light color, some white, and some yellow, and streak it in on the rendering over the highlight area. The different chalks will blend by themselves as they are streaked onto the paper. Go back to the chalk and pick up some of the medium color; streak it over the body of the object. Repeat again with the dark chalk mixed with a little violet and apply this to the shade areas. By now the rendering will look messy (figure 8-10).

Remove the frisket paper and use a kneaded eraser to pick up most of the overlap chalk from around the rendering (figure 8-11). With a pink pearl eraser, erase and clean up the residue of chalk. Then erase chalk to

8-9. Ultrasonic Humidifier. A soft, absorbent paper was used with this chalk technique. First the blacks and darks were put in with markers, over which chalk was applied and removed.

8-10. Ultrasonic Humidifier. Frisket paper was fitted and cut around the body of the project. Then chalk was applied, working left to right, light to dark.

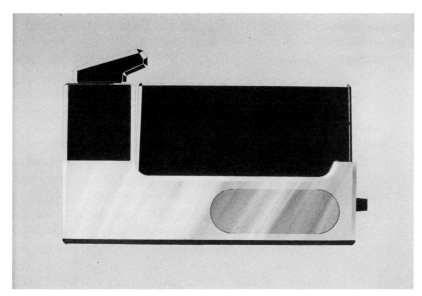

get highlights on the object. Now there will be a crisp chalk rendering with dull dark areas, since the chalk is over the marker. To correct this, spray a workable fixative over the entire rendering. This will melt the marker, allowing it to come through the chalk (be absorbed by the chalk), giving good darks again (figure 8-12). This will also intensify the colors of the chalk. Details are added with fine linework and transfer lettering. Some small highlights can be painted into this rendering (figure 8-13), but extensive detail work over the chalk is very difficult.

Using chalk for a simple background involves essentially the same process. In figures 8-14 and 8-15, wax adhesive painter's tape was used to mask around the background area to keep chalk off the product and confined to the rectangle. Powdered chalk was rubbed over the background area, working from left to right, light to dark. Finally, the paper tape mask was removed, and a light coat of spray fixative was applied to keep the rendering from smearing.

8-11. Ultrasonic Humidifier. The frisket was removed and the edges of the chalk area cleaned up with an eraser.

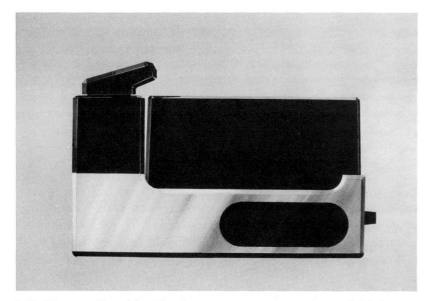

8-12. Ultrasonic Humidifier. The whole drawing was sprayed with a washable fixative, causing the chalk to be absorbed in the dark areas.

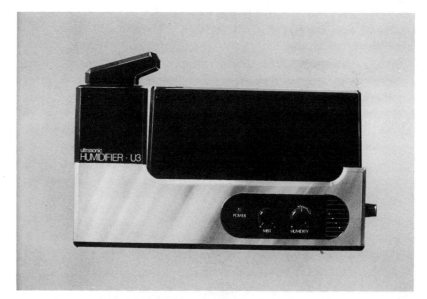

8-13. Ultrasonic Humidifier. Details were added with fine liner and press type.

CHALK RENDERINGS

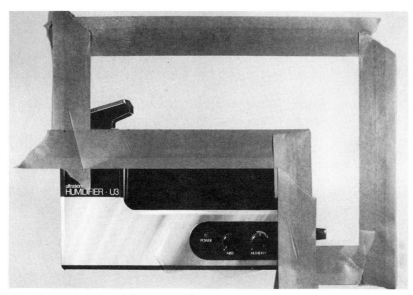

8-14. Ultrasonic Humidifier. Wax adhesive painter's tape was used to mask out a background area.

8-15. Ultrasonic Humidifier. A colored chalk background was rubbed in and the wax removed.

This dry chalk technique is very quick and effective for quick form studies but is limited in its ability to show great detail or surface development.

Dissolved Chalk Background Rendering

By dissolving powdered chalk on a pad saturated with a solvent like Flo-master cleanser or lighter fluid, the chalk can be streaked down with an effect similar to a thin coat of opaque paint. This is a striking effect but provides little control. For that reason it is most commonly used in backgrounds where a simple mask can be made to control it and where there is no need for detail (figure 8-16). One way to expedite this technique is to incorporate the object into the background and carve it out with some strong linework and shadows. The chalk is handled the same way as with dry powdered chalk wash, except that the cotton pad is wet with solvent. The procedure is outlined below. It is quick and often very bold and dramatic. Because of the dramatic effect, this technique is not always considered appropriate for presentations.

1. On the light pencil drawing, darken all lines except those that will be highlights.
2. Mask around the background and object so that the wet chalk can be applied over both in long, vertical strokes.
3. Stroke the light values through the leading edge of the product, primarily toward the light source of the object.
4. Progressively darken the chalk color as you move away from the leading edge. The shade side of the object receives the darkest, coolest colors.
5. Remove the mask and strengthen the linework. Paint in white highlights and add details with marker or designer's gouache.

There are many variations on this technique. Inks and dyes may be substituted for the chalk and solvent for a similar effect. The masking procedure may be expanded for a more elaborate rendering or reduced to a minimum, letting the background become just a part of the shade side of an object.

8-16. Taboret. For this rendering a mask was put around the background and the object; then color was wiped on with a cotton pad. Once the color was dry and the mask removed, bold linework was put in to define the form; finally, highlights were added to the front edges.

CHALK RENDERINGS

151

Vellum

Vellum paper has characteristics that make it a unique rendering surface. Vellum is a translucent, nonabsorbent paper with a soft finish. Markers flow very freely on vellum and blend easily because the color "surface-dries" on the paper. However, the colors are not as bright or intense as with standard marker paper because are not absorbed into the paper. The soft finish on the paper also provides enough tooth for pencil and chalk to hold well. For these reasons, vellum is a very workable surface. Marker color can be picked up or blended even after it has dried. Also, pencil and chalk can be used extensively. The translucency of vellum is its unique feature. Marker and chalk can be applied to the back side of the paper and they will show through, lightened or toned down slightly by the paper fiber.

Rendering with Vellum

A rendering will be started on vellum in the same manner as with standard marker paper. Highlight areas can be toned from the back of the paper with pale chalk, surfaces can be modulated with chalk on the front or back sides, and, most important, shade and shadow areas can be deepened and toned by applying marker to the back of the paper. After the rendering is completed, spraying the back of the paper with flat, white paint will intensify the colors and brighten the rendering.

Vellum offers one other advantage over other papers: masking is made simpler because almost any tape can be put down and pulled off vellum without ripping the surface. Scotch transparent tape is a particularly effective masking material because it is thin, enabling markers to move over it freely. It is easier to position than most other tapes because lines can be seen through it, and the adhesive is strong, thus preventing any bleeding by the marker color. Used on other paper surfaces, this tape will cause the paper to tear. It can be used successfully only on vellum. For other papers use Scotch low-tack tape.

The sequence and application technique of markers, chalk, and pencil is essentially the same as with rendering on other papers, with one exception. Because the markers dry slowly on the vellum and may be dissolved and blended with successive application of markers, or even wiped off with a solvent, there is a new aspect to marker handling.

The remelting of marker color means that a light marker applied over a darker one will pick up some of the darker color, thus lightening the area. This can be annoying if you are used to more absorbent papers on which a light marker will only tone or further darken an area. However, this remelting is very helpful for blending. By putting down the dark marker over one third of an area and stroking a light marker over the entire surface, the dark marker will melt and blend over the entire area resulting in a nice gradation or modulation. By consistently applying darker markers over lighter markers, this color pickup is not noticeable and the melting that occurs tends to soften edges, eliminating the characteristic marker streaks found when rendering on other papers. If you wish to darken an area slightly without layering or blending the markers, turn the paper over and apply a dark color to the back side of the area you wish to darken. In this way there is no melting or blending, only a controlled darkening, or color shift.

Presentation Techniques

In addition to these various rendering techniques, the presentation of renderings is worth examining. It is the presentation that sets up the rendering. A weak rendering that is well presented may get more attention and consideration than a good rendering with a weak presentation. There are many ways to present design concepts and renderings. Almost every design organization has its own method and style. Most of their styles are variations on storyboards and can range from very simple mounting of renderings on cardboard to a slide presentation of work very carefully laid out and photographed with a consistent format, typography, and style.

Storyboards

Storyboards are series of plates that together form a presentation of a design problem or solution. Storyboards take presentation drawings, such as renderings, and present them in a more formal, serious manner than simply handing them to a client or tacking them to a wall (figures 8-17 and 8-18 and C16 in the color section). By mounting the work on mat-board you are, in a sense, framing it; it becomes a more formal statement about an idea without actually being perceived as a work of art (which would be the message if it were framed).

8-17 and 8-18. Exhibit Design, William Hansen, Kitzing, Inc., Chicago, IL. These storyboards show two variations on the same design. By keeping the layout, colors, and technique the same, both boards have a similar visual impact.

SPECIALIZED RENDERING TECHNIQUES

The degree of organization and the amount of design that goes into the boards themselves depends upon the nature of the presentation and the audience. With product design the presentation is generally informal, and the client usually understands the product well. The storyboards may therefore be simply renderings taped to pieces of illustration or mat-board, all of which are the same size. There are occasions in which the audience is not familiar with the product and there is no opportunity for verbal explanation. Here more formal storyboards are required.

The planning and design considerations that go into making a storyboard presentation are outlined below. They may be followed very loosely and simply for a casual presentation or with great care and precision for a formal presentation.

There is no discussion of photographic techniques offered here, but you should be aware that photostats of renderings, slide shows, and photographs can always be incorporated into a presentation.

Planning

The most direct way to plan a sequence of storyboards is to make a brief script of the information you want to convey. A verbal statement of the visual information not only helps you plan your drawings, but also directs your presentation to the main design points and ensures that you cover all the essential aspects of the design. Naturally, not all of the information about a design can be presented on storyboards, but you want to present a complete picture of the product so that it can be understood and seen from the designer's point of view. At first, all you will need is a rough outline of the information you want to present in order to plan the individual boards. A more detailed script will be developed as the storyboards are being prepared, and eventually title boards and brief descriptions from the script will be added to the storyboards to supplement the renderings.

Board Sequence

The rough outline needs to be broken down into segments. Each segment will contain the information for one storyboard. You should have roughly the same amount of information on each board planned

8-19. In this chair design storyboard, the environment is shown but in a very subordinate way, so that it serves as a background as well as provides information about the use of the chair.

for the presentation. Once the verbal information is broken down a visual image needs to be planned to illustrate that information best. Perhaps the best way to describe this is to list a possible sequence of boards and the information they might have:

1. Rendering of the product with title and brief verbal description of function. This first board introduces the design in a very general way. We see the form, color, and style and can make associations with similar products from our experience. This is perhaps the most important board in the sequence for presenting a new design.
2. Rendering of auxiliary products or various uses of the product with labels identifying each part or use. On the second board the product's environment is described, as well as the system of products that relate to it (figure 8-19).
3. Technical drawing of the product showing dimensions and major parts and elements. This board gives an idea of the engineering and manufacturing processes included in the new product and perhaps an idea of the production costs.

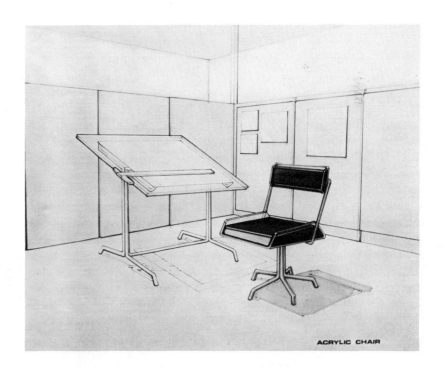

ACRYLIC CHAIR

4. Graphics and specific layout of the controls on the product. This board goes into detail about the product. It gives an idea of the typography and graphic design as well as the logic of the controls and human factors of operating the product (C16 in the color section).

5. Line drawings of mechanical details and special parts. Here the viewer is shown the completeness of the design and the unique functioning of some of the detail elements. This enables the viewer to imagine using the product and thus understand it more as a real product.

6. Rendering of a different view or a styling variation on the product. By offering a different view or change of style for the product, it remains a flexible concept open to refinement and change. The degree to which a styling variation differs from the rendering on the first board will indicate how much latitude there is for discussion of changes.

Any one of these six storyboards may require more than one board for all the information. In addition, other boards may be added for packaging or other considerations. Your aim is to plan a series of visual images to communicate the major concerns in product design—form, use, manufacture, technology, graphics, safety, and control.

Layout

Once the visual information has been planned, an overall layout for the storyboards needs to be made. Then a good organizational pattern must be worked out that can be applied to each board to provide a consistent, uniform appearance from board to board.

The most common layout for a series of storyboards is to have them all the same size and in a row. This produces a flexible, effective, convenient presentation. However, it is not always possible to have all the drawings close to the same size so that they look right on the same size board. When this is the case, you must establish a basic unit that can be multiplied for larger drawings (e.g., 8″ x 10″, 16″ x 20″, or 24″ x 30″), or set a standard height (e.g., 14″ x 17″, 17″ x 22″, or 17″ x 28″) and let the width vary. With either method the fewer the number of sizes the better the unity. Of course, more elaborate customized layouts can be designed. However, they tend to look contrived and inappropriate compared with the simplicity and directness usually desired in a design presentation.

Applying a grid to each of the storyboards is similar to designing the page layout for a book, but since there are only a few "pages" the process can be simplified a great deal. Storyboards contain three basic elements: a title, an image, and some descriptive copy. By keeping these elements consistent in size and placement, only a few basic grid measurements are needed to lay out the boards. The first measurement is the margin. It is customary to leave at least 2 inches of margin on a board, and slightly more on the bottom (2½ inches). The heading is usually put flush left to the margin, either at the top or the bottom of the board. The image usually fills the space inside the margin from side to side but may vary in height, allowing the bottom margin to increase. The copy is set in a block that can be positioned about the board. By keeping the copy block the same width it can be positioned in vacant or dead space to fill out a composition. A simple guide for positioning elements on a board is to use a consistent unit of measurement for spacing and to line up elements so that they have common margins. The only exception is the first, or introductory, board. You may wish to create a strong visual attraction to this board by altering the grid layout, adding some decorative elements such as a bold color line, or putting the headline type at an angle.

Auxiliary Drawings

Because renderings are time-consuming, you will not want to produce renderings for all the storyboards in a presentation. Line drawings, orthographic drawings, and sketches can be used to illustrate the details of a design concept. This presents some problems, however: each storyboard must appear to be part of the same presentation and each must have the same visual impact. To do this you must reconsider the traditional conventions used to make these auxiliary drawings and look for ways to add bold linework and color to these drawings. For example, the traditional method for doing orthographic and engineering drawings provides a great deal of technical information about a product but is visually very weak and difficult for many people to understand. In a presentation it is not necessary to go into great detail about technical information. Therefore, an engineering drawing can be simplified and enhanced for greater visual impact. If detailed technical information is required, an engineering drawing may be supplied in addition to the storyboard presentation.

To *simplify* a drawing some of the hidden lines and dimensioning may be eliminated. The views of the product can be rearranged for a logical, compact fit on the paper. The first step in *enhancing* a drawing is to strengthen and exaggerate the line weights. The perimeter lines of the object can be made very bold with other lines increasing in weight respective to their importance (refer to the section on line weights, chapter 3). Once the line weights have been made stronger, some gray values, or even pale color, may be added to the drawing. It is not necessary to make an orthographic rendering. Flat areas of color will give the drawing enough impact to separate it from the page so that the product shape and information are easy to read. Another use of color is to dimension and label the orthographic drawing with colored ink, rather than black. This helps separate object lines from dimension lines, making the object easier to understand, as well as adding some visual excitement to the board.

Another type of auxiliary drawing is a line sketch. This is usually a freehand drawing showing a particular aspect of the product or its use. These sketches are filled out nicely by including a sketch of the user or environment. To give impact to a line sketch, tone the drawing with some marker color or chalk color. Do not "color in" the entire drawing; just suggest color in the main interest areas (usually the product) and let a lot of the white of the paper show. Again, strong linework and careful composition of the image are important.

Backup Materials

A final consideration when producing storyboards or any presentation is how to present backup materials, such as material samples, photographs, prototypes, or models. Most of the time this is not a problem; the backup materials can simply be placed on a table or stand to be examined by the client. However, in a more formal presentation it is often inappropriate to pass things around among a group of people. Backup materials may also distract the viewer and take his attention away from the presentation. Controlling the presentation and directing the viewer's attention is problematic for many people. For this reason be very critical of what materials you plan to show and decide whether they should be shown during or after the presentation. Interior designers solve this problem very neatly. They make a storyboard and include swatches of materials on the board itself. In this way the materials can be presented and discussed but are not readily available to distract attention. They may be examined more closely after the presentation. An effective way to present models is to show a sequence of slides demonstrating the model, then bring the model out after the presentation for examination. When booklets or other handout materials are to be used, be sure to have enough for everyone. Make the presentation of the design concept *before* passing out the materials. That way you are sure the message is delivered without distraction or confusion.

The accompanying examples of storyboards will give you an idea of how attention to layout and a simple, direct approach to handling elements make handsome, effective presentations.

A final consideration when putting together storyboards is how to mount the renderings and drawings.

Mounting

There are three standard materials used to mount drawings: mounting tissue, tape, and spray adhesive or rubber cement.

Mounting Tissue

Mounting tissue, the most effective of these materials, comes in two styles: a dry-mount tissue and a sticky adhesive sheet. Both styles are cut to cover the back of the drawing paper, and the drawing is mounted by sandwiching the tissue between the mount board and the drawing paper. Dry-mount tissue requires a tack iron to position and hold the tissue in place; then the "sandwich" is put into a hot press which melts the dry adhesive and bonds the drawing to the mount board. Because the adhesive covers the entire drawing sheet and a press is used, wrinkles are eliminated from the drawing paper and the mounting is very smooth and permanent. Adhesive sheets require very careful handling, especially on thin drawing papers. The adhesive sheet is positioned on the back of the drawing and trimmed to size. Then the drawing is mounted on the board. This tissue requires no press but is very susceptible to trapped dirt behind the drawing and to crooked positionings. Both types of tissues come with explicit directions and helpful tips. When done correctly the mounting actually improves the appearance of the drawing.

Tape

The most effective use of tape mounting is to use a thin, black, ¼-inch tape and tape the edges down all around the drawing paper. This leaves a bold black line around the drawing, which can be attractive. It also holds down all the edges, which eliminates wrinkling and curling of the edges. Double-stick tape can also be used behind each corner of a drawing to hold it in place. This is the least attractive way to mount paper as wrinkles, curled edges, and sagging are always a problem.

Adhesives

A third popular method of mounting is to use spray adhesive or rubber cement. Both work well on heavy stock. However, for thin marker paper the results can be disastrous. Because all papers contain some moisture they expand and contract depending upon the ambient humidity. By mounting a thin paper to a board with spray adhesive you can almost guarantee that large bubbles will appear in the paper that will not go away. Also, if any of the spray gets on the front surface of the drawing or mount board, it will attract dirt like iron filings to a magnet and will be almost impossible to clean. Sprays are very useful for mounting heavy papers, and when handled carefully, they are effective and neat. However, they do not work for mounting large, thin paper. Rubber cement poses different problems. It tends to be messy, and on thin paper it will stain and discolor a drawing in a short time.

When mounting your work, dry-mount tissue gives the nicest results. However, it requires equipment and is permanent. Edge taping is the next preferable method. It is fast and nonpermanent.

By way of summary: since a rendering is intended for display, you cannot consider it finished until it is mounted or copied on a slide and ready for presentation. To keep attention focused on the rendering, keep the mounting and presentation as simple and direct as possible. Be careful of details, but do not overdo the presentation style.

Glossary of Materials and Methods

Brushes

Paintbrushes consist of bristles, a metal ferrule, and a wooden handle. The bristles are the most important part, so you want to get a good-quality sable brush. Sable bristles keep a tip well, carry and hold a good body of pigment, and are responsive. The brush is primarily used for highlighting and lettering, both of which require a fine point (0 or 00). You may want to get a fine lettering brush as well. A lettering brush has a chiseled tip that produces an even, flat stroke for lettering or wide highlights.

Colored Pencils

Colored pencils are very good for detailing small areas, adding highlights, and adding a color tone to part of a drawing. A fairly soft, wax-base pencil and a wide selection of colors are recommended for rendering. Three brands that are all of good quality and readily available are Berol Prismacolor, Venus Spectra-color, and Eberhard-Faber Colorama. The pencils need to be handled with care as the leads will break easily. Dropping an unsharpened pencil on a hard floor may crack the lead inside; a rough pencil sharpener may continually "chew up" the point. An electric pencil sharpener is very handy for keeping a good point.

When pencils are being sharpened frequently (as in rendering) the electric pencil sharpener saves time. When purchasing colored pencils select a color palette from both the warm and cool ranges. Accent colors like violet and pink should also be included. Check the end of the pencil to see if the lead is well centered; if not, the pencil will not sharpen to a good point.

Colored pencils are essentially transparent and may be used in three ways. The first method uses a sharp point to tighten up edges, to add highlights, or to put in thin accent lines. These thin lines are often ruled in along a triangle or guide. A helpful technique when ruling is to twirl the pencil as you draw it along the edge. This keeps a point and prevents the line from getting fat and vague.

A white pencil is commonly used for highlights along edges and in details. In dark areas, however, a silver pencil will do a better job; the white pencil is dulled by the dark marker dye while the reflective silver picks up room light and gives added sparkle to the highlight. A thin line of warm accent color (e.g., light yellow) along the highlight edge will crisp up the highlight and make the surface seem more reflective as well as add a tint of color that helps create a sense of light and atmosphere about the rendering. A cool accent color (e.g., lilac) can be put in the shade area along the halo to crisp up and cool the back edge of the rendering.

The second manner in which colored pencils are used is to tone an area. By using an underhand grip on the pencil the side of the lead can be rubbed over an area imparting a thin, transparent tone which can alter the color, put a glow on a surface, or warm or cool areas. Be sure to have a smooth surface under the marker paper as any texture will be picked up by the pencils.

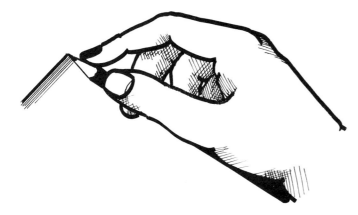

G-1. An underhand grip can be used for a variety of toning effects.

The third use for colored pencils is to add small details. A detail may be built up with successive layers of the transparent color, working in highlights and shade areas as you go. By blending the colors together with a white, light gray, or cream pencil and then adding a final layer of color, the intensity is increased and a smooth, uniform surface is left. The edges of the detail can be tightened up with a fine, dark pencil or pen. Markers can also be worked over colored pencil. They melt the pencil and blend it which dulls and tints the pencil color. Do not overdo it with the markers, however. The area will become muddy and the pencil will have to be cleaned out of the marker tip by stroking the marker on a sheet of scratch paper; otherwise the wax from the pencils may clog the marker's nib.

Drawing Pencils and Leads

Two types of drawing pencils are available: the common wood lead pencil and the mechanical pencil that accepts a variety of different leads. The leads for mechanical pencils range from hard to soft and from a large to a very fine point (.3mm). These fine leads are nice for drafting and linework as they do not need sharpening. The larger leads are better for drawing as they can put down more graphite quickly and with a variety of lines.

Pencil leads come in a range of hardness from 6B (very soft) to 9H (very hard). A middle range of pencil leads works well for most rendering. Soft leads, such as 2B or HB, produce bold, dark lines for lettering and some shading. F and H are medium-soft leads which keep a fine point for detailing and tightening up lettering. A 2H lead is medium-hard, the same as a common lead pencil, and is good for light-line drawings and layout work. A pencil with a very soft lead, 6B, can give a very dark line and is good for quick value studies. Because soft leads put down so much graphite they also smear easily if you run your hand over them. You may wish to slip a piece of paper under your palm to prevent smudging.

Ellipse Guides

A circle in perspective is drawn as an ellipse. Depending upon the angle from which you are viewing the circle it will appear as anywhere from a very narrow ellipse to a very full "round" ellipse. Ellipse guides come in a series of 5° increments, from a narrow 10° ellipse to a wide 80° ellipse. The guides also come in two sets, one from ⅛ inch to 2 inches and the other from 2⅛ inches to 4 inches. Having access to both sets of ellipse guides is very helpful when rendering because freehand ellipses are difficult to draw and seldom convincing.

Erasers

A number of different erasers are available. However, only two types are needed in rendering: a kneaded eraser and a "pink pearl." The kneaded eraser is soft and pliable and will remove large amounts of pencil or chalk from a drawing. When the eraser becomes "dirty," knead it clean. The advantages of the kneaded eraser are that it does not leave crumbs and can be shaped to a point to pick out details.

The "pink pearl" is a soft rubber eraser that removes lines the kneaded eraser will not remove. It comes in varying degrees of hardness, and because all hard erasers tend to rough up the paper, I recommend you use a soft pink eraser. The pink eraser may also be used to "draw" light lines in chalked areas by erasing lines in the chalk. This eraser is cleaned by rubbing it on a piece of scrap paper.

Erasing Shields

A typical erasing shield is a small rectangular piece of metal with a variety of shaped holes cut into it through which you can erase. For rendering you may often wish to erase up to or along an edge. To do this, a piece of paper may be layed down as a shield.

Flexible Curves

Flexible curves are strips of metal or plastic that may be bent into almost any gentle curve. These guides allow you to rule a fine or broad line on irregular contours. Kinks commonly develop in these curves when they are handled roughly or when you try to make a tight corner. Once a kink develops, the curve is of little use for accurate lines, so handle them carefully. To use the curve, twist it into roughly the desired shape and position it on the paper. Holding it firmly with one hand, adjust it to the exact curve you want and rule your line with the other hand.

Flo-master Inks

Flo-master inks come in dispenser cans to refill Flo-master pens. By squeezing the ink directly from the dispenser onto a cotton pad, the ink can be smeared onto a masked area for a bright background. These inks come in a basic range of bright colors and black. They are so bright that the colors should be mixed and black added to them to tone them down for backgrounds. As you might expect, these inks are very messy to use and require practice to be handled successfully.

Guides

Another way to control an otherwise loose application of color is to use a guide. This is simply a shaped pattern that guides the marker or other tool along its edge. The most common guides are triangle, circle, and ellipse guides and T squares. When used with markers the guides must be held slightly above the paper surface so the dye will not bleed under the guide. This may be done by taping a thin piece of cardboard to the underside of the guide just in from the edge. Some people tape dimes under the guides to "lift" them. The marker is then either drawn along the edge of the guide or butted up to it in a series of rapid strokes. A very convenient guide for marking straight lines is a piece of mat-board. You can run the marker along the edge without the dye bleeding underneath. Mat-board is also disposable, so there is no need to clean the edges after each use.

Guides are also very effective when spraying color to block an area or control an edge when spraying color. Note that the further from the paper surface the guide is held the fuzzier the edge of the line becomes. This is an advantage that masks do not have.

Bridges

A bridge is a specialized guide for use with paintbrushes. Bridges are usually straight with feet at either end so that they will span over the drawing without touching it. The edge is raised high enough off the paper surface so that the ferrule of the brush runs along the edge. The fingers lightly run across the top of the bridge to control the touch of the brush on the paper, thus determining the line width. To achieve shaped lines another guide may be laid on the bridge with the desired shape extending over the edge of the bridge to run the brush along.

Light Table

A light table is a useful tool for refining, tightening up, or modifying a line drawing. It consists of a series of lights arranged under a white translucent surface. Preliminary line drawings may be taped down and the lines "projected" through a clean sheet laid over the drawing. Using a light pencil the projected lines may be traced or changed as desired. With the light table off the lines from the underlay vanish, leaving a new drawing free from distracting lines and ready for further work.

Marker Papers

Three characteristics of paper are important when selecting paper for marker rendering: you want a paper that takes the marker well and shows a clean, bright color; you want little bleeding of the marker stroke; and you want the marker to dry quickly. These tend to be conflicting requirements. For instance, an absorbent paper that dries quickly and shows colors brightly will tend to bleed a lot. Three types of paper work well; each has its own advantages and disadvantages.

Vellum is a translucent paper that does not bleed at all and has the unique advantage of being able to be worked from the back side. That is, marker strokes on the back side of the paper will show through, but with a subdued tone. For example, a black marker used on the back side of the paper will show through as a #7 gray. This is effective for putting in shadows and for darkening an area. Vellum also has a soft surface that accepts chalk and colored pencil well. The drawbacks to vellum are a slow drying time for the markers and the fact that colors are not as strong as on more absorbent papers.

Marker layout paper is a thin, white, fairly opaque paper that is made to accept marker dye with little bleeding. The colors will be strong, but light. However this paper does not accept chalk well.

Colored marker paper is heavy paper that takes markers, chalk, and pencil. It is very absorbent and causes some bleeding of the marker, so all fine work must be done with pencil, ink, and chalk.

There are a number of high-quality papers in each category. Individual preference and rendering style should determine your choice. The following papers are suggested for their good marker-handling qualities:

Vellum

Art-Vel
Hunt/Bienfang
Statesville, NC 28677

Ogilvie Press, Inc.
95 Industrial Ave. E.
Clifton, NJ 07010

Marker Layout Paper

Graphics
Hunt/Bienfang
Statesville, NC 28677

M-3
Letraset USA, Inc.
40 Eisenhower Dr.
Paramus, NJ 07652

Colored Marker Paper

Crescent Drawing & Illustration Boards
Crescent Cardboard Co.
P.O. Box XD
100 W. Willow Road
Wheeling, IL 60090

Mi-Tientes
Morilla Inc.
211 Bauers St.
Holyoke, MA 01040

Masks

Masking is an effective technique for getting crisp edges around quickly rendered areas of a drawing; it is done for either marker, chalk, or dyes (e.g., Flo-master). Masking is used in rendering in two ways: to block out, and keep white, a small area that can be rendered around and over, and to mask around a large area that can then be rendered quickly and loosely.

Unless the area to be masked has straight edges and sharp corners on which masking tapes can be applied directly, the mask will need to be cut and shaped to the desired contour. To avoid cutting through the marker paper either render on a heavy board (e.g., illustration board) or precut the mask before applying it to the rendering. Precutting is easily done by using a translucent mask material (frisket or tracing paper), laying it over the rendering, and tracing the lines to be cut. Lay the translucent mask material over a smooth cutting surface and carefully cut along the trace lines. Position the mask on the rendering and apply the color.

When markers are used the mask must adhere firmly to the paper at the edge or the marker dye will bleed under the mask. The adhesive may be discolored by the marker base and leave stains or may be too tacky and tear the paper or pull up the color under it. Several good masking materials are available. Frisket

is perhaps the best for cutting out shaped areas. Tracing paper works well when layered over the drawing if you are only stroking away from the mask or if you are using dry chalk. Any unwanted chalk may be removed with a pink pearl eraser.

For straight edges and angular corners many tapes can be used. Scotch tape is very good on vellum but will tear marker paper. It is also easy to cut corners and shaped details by lifting the edge and lightly cutting the tape with a sharp #11 X-acto blade. On marker and layout paper a light-tack drafting tape (a tape that will hold its position but not tear the paper when pulled off) works. If there is too much adhesive, stick the tape to your drafting table and pull it up again. This may be repeated until the desired light tack is achieved. Another good mask for marker paper is the wax-backed painter's mask found in most hardware stores. It has a light tack, yet bonds well at the edge. The wax does not leave a residue on the paper.

Morgue File

A morgue file is a convenient source file of reference materials for both the beginner and the experienced renderer. It may contain photographs of things you wish to draw from, examples of specific details or materials that are troublesome to render, or images of people and support elements to put into a rendering for scale and interest. The following is a suggested list for building a file. Be very selective in what you put into your file and continue to build and edit it. You will find it a valuable tool:

- a collection of photographs of products to draw from and refer to for details, reflections, highlights, and transitions. Select a clear, well-defined photograph rather than an overly dramatic or shadowed one.
- examples of rendering and sketching techniques from both printed material and original work. These can be a source for growth and help demonstrate how others solved certain problems.
- a people file of both casual sketches and photographic examples. Some anatomical and ergonomic references are also helpful here. Avoid excessively stylized and distorted fashion illustrations.
- a general catch-all file of things that interest you.
- a file of technical drawings and diagrams.

Opaque White

Opaque white is a water-base paint that covers markers, pencil, and ink without bleeding. It may be used with a brush, a technical pen, or an airbrush.

The two main uses for opaque white are to put in highlights and to put in light details. When light details are desired on a dark ground, the opaque white is put down with the light color over it. A note of caution: if you are detailing with a water-base, fineline dark pen, putting white opaque over it will melt the color, which in turn will contaminate the white opaque. Always thin the opaque to the consistency of heavy cream so that it flows well from the brush or pen; it has a tendency to thicken and glob on.

Pastels and Chalk

The extent to which pastels and chalk can be used in a marker rendering depends upon the paper being used. Chalk will not adhere to hard, smooth papers like marker paper, but will take very nicely to toothy, or soft papers like canson or diazo paper. Chalks are generally used for backgrounds, for toning areas, and for adding highlights or glare to a rendering.

Chalks can be used dry or dissolved with thinner on a cotton pad. As a dry medium, the chalk may be stroked directly onto the paper from the square stick. This leaves a hard edge to the chalk which is advantageous when rendering highlights and glare. To tone an area, the chalk should be powdered by scraping with a blade and rubbed on the rendering with a cotton pad. When rubbing the chalk, it is helpful to use masks. An eraser may be used to clean up edges or "draw" light lines in the chalk.

To use chalk as a wet medium, powder it and use a cotton pad dipped in thinner (rubber cement thinner or lighter fluid) to pick up the chalk and stroke it on the rendering. When used wet, chalk is difficult to remove, so careful masking is important.

There are a few guidelines for using chalk in a marker rendering that you will want to observe:

- Like markers, chalks should be applied directly without repeated handling. Put a stroke down and leave it. Overworking an area makes for a smudged, muddy rendering.
- When chalk colors are mixed, they lose their brilliance. This is to your advantage in backgrounds where more subdued colors are desired. Also, incomplete mixing causes streaking, which can be a nice effect. For highlights and toning, however, keep the colors pure and bright.
- Chalks smudge easily and will melt and muddy when markers are applied over them. They also tend to clog marker tips. Therefore, put the chalk on a rendering at the very end, after all the other work is done. Spraying fixative over chalk darkens the color and in some cases softens the marker enough to

allow it to blend with the chalk. When this occurs the chalk color is no longer visible.
- If chalks need to be applied to a marker paper, the surface must be prepared with a fine abrasive. Rubbing the paper with talc, even over markers, will allow the chalk to adhere to the surface better.
- To remove large amounts of chalk, use a kneaded eraser and blot up most of the chalk. Then use a soft pink eraser to remove the final bits of color.
- Chalk sticks may be shaped on fine sandpaper to control their width and to keep a sharp edge.

Rapidographs

Rapidograph is a brand name commonly used to refer to all hollow-point technical drawing pens. These pens come in a range of point sizes from .13 mm to 2 mm. The very fine points are designated by zeros, 5 x 0 ("00000") being the finest, and increasing in size through 4 x 0 ("0000"), 3 x 0, "00" and "0," all the way to 6. They all produce a very sharp, uniform line. Used primarily for technical drawing, these pens are also excellent for detailing a rendering. They use a waterproof black ink. Although colored inks are available, the difficulty of changing inks makes using them impractical. You may, however, want to consider keeping one pen for use with white ink for some highlights and white linework. The major problem with Rapidographs is that the ink tends to dry and clog the tip. There is little you can do to prevent this, although the newer pens have good seals in the caps and dry out very slowly.

T Squares

A T square slides along the edge of your drawing board, allowing you to rule a series of horizontal, parallel lines. Triangles can be set on the edge of a T square to rule vertical or angular lines. It is important that the T square have a raised or beveled edge to prevent bleeding under it as you rule lines or stroke markers along its edge.

Thinners and Solvents

Solvents such as rubber cement thinner, naphtha, acetone, lighter fluid, and xylene are very volatile and can be dangerous. A spill-proof dispenser, such as an "oil can" rubber-cement-thinner dispenser, is recommended to prevent spilling. Solvents are useful for wetting a cloth or cotton pad to clean marker dye off drafting tools. They are also used for special effects and for blending markers and chalk. When rendering on vellum, a solvent pad can be used to "erase" or pick up marker color from the paper. Some art material companies offer special solvents for their products in prepackaged dispensers, although two common universal solvents for markers are rubber cement thinner and lighter fluid.

Transfer Paper

To transfer a line drawing to an opaque surface (illustration board or canson), a transfer sheet—a sheet similar to carbon paper—is slipped between the drawing and the new surface. The line drawing is then redrawn using firm pressure, causing the chalky powder on the transfer paper to mark the lines on the opaque surface. The lines of this transfer drawing are not permanent and may easily be erased. They also resist smudging, making them clean and easy to work with. An alternate method of transferring a drawing is to rub the back side with colored chalk or colored pencil (metallic Prismacolor works well). This is a more time-consuming technique, and the chalk method can be messy. Both the transfer paper lines and the chalk lines are easy to remove from the paper surface and when drawn over with marker tend to dissolve. The metallic pencil lines do not readily dissolve, but they are light and can only be seen when looked at from an angle; they are not evident in the final rendering.

Triangles

There are two basic triangles—a 45° and a 30°-60°. You will need one of each. Aside from the traditional drafting tasks, triangles are useful as straightedges for tightening up a rendering and as guides to run markers along. Of the two triangles, the 30°-60° is the most convenient for rendering because it covers less surface area for the same length hypotenuse. Therefore, it is less awkward to move about the drawing board when used as a straightedge.

The transparent acrylic triangles have two advantages over other triangles: first, you can see through them, making positioning easier; second, the edge does not crack or get sticky when it is cleaned with marker solvent. As with all guides the edge of the triangle should be raised or beveled to prevent bleeding.

It is advisable to have a number of different size triangles. The most commonly used is a 12-inch triangle, measured along the longest leg. This size is sufficient for most rendering and layout work.

Appendix A
Selecting Markers

This appendix briefly reviews the general characteristics of markers and the various marker brands available to the designer. I have not attempted any direct comparisons of different marker brands as availability and personal preference will better determine your choice. The range of colors offered by each marker brand varies greatly. You will find that some sets have very bright, intense colors that are good for graphic design and layout work, while other sets include a wide range of muted tones that are necessary for rendering and architectural work. In general, however, each marker company offers a wide enough selection of markers for most product rendering needs. The deciding factor in selecting a marker brand may be how well that brand suits your personal work habits. The most common considerations are how juicy the markers are and how fast they flow; whether the markers are comfortable in your hand; whether the marker stand is convenient; and whether you prefer to work with a large nib (e.g., AD Marker) or a smaller nib (e.g., Mecanorma).

Testing Markers

When purchasing markers, test them on the same type of paper on which you will be rendering, since different papers accept color formulations differently. This in turn affects the appearance of the color. On absorbent papers like layout bond, the colors are deeper, and subtle distinctions or changes of colors are more difficult to discern. On thin marker papers, however, the colors are lighter and subtleties, such as a slight bluish cast to a red marker, are more apparent. The best all-around marker paper may be a 15 lb. natural tracing paper. This is a white paper that has no fluorescents, coatings, transparentizers, or other additives that will affect the markers.

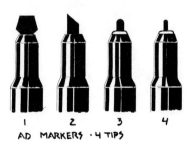

1   2   3   4
AD MARKERS · 4 TIPS

FRONT   SIDE
MECANORMA

WEDGE
PANTONE

A-1. Various marker tips are illustrated here. The first four are the interchangeable tips offered by AD markers. The next two show the unique shape of the Mecanorma Markers. The last tip, illustrated by a Pantone Marker, shows a typical wedge nib.

Chemical Base of Markers

The chemical base used to formulate the colors makes some difference when using markers. The most common base is aromatic xylene which is toxic and may annoy some users. However, there is such a slight exposure when using markers that average room ventilation clears the air. Alcohol-base markers have a strong odor, but do not seem irritating to most people. Water-base markers have no odor at all, but are unsatisfactory for most rendering tasks. (More on this below.)

The major concerns over the chemical base of markers are drying time, permanence, and degree of bleeding. (The absorbency of the paper is also a factor in drying time and bleeding.) Both xylene- and alcohol-base markers dry rapidly, yet allow time for slight blending. They will also bleed a great deal on absorbent papers. Both produce permanent colors, but the colors of alcohol-base markers are slightly more vivid. Water-base markers are the slowest to dry, and you may find yourself smearing wet color with your hand or a drawing tool. This, combined with their tendency to "slip" over oil, wax, or even fingerprints, and to be smudged by the moisture of your hand, gives them a very limited use in rendering. However, they bleed very little.

Bleeding can also occur when a fine line is "washed" over with a broad-tip marker of the same chemical base. The solvent in the broad tip dissolves the fine line causing it to bleed. To avoid this either put fine lines in last or use a water-base fine line under the xylene- and alcohol-base markers.

Using Markers with Triangles

When markers are used with plastic triangles to draw straight lines, the dark markers leave color on the edge of the triangle. This color can be picked up on your hands and then smudged back on the rendering, or by successive lighter markers. These lighter markers will be "contaminated" and streak when they are used. To avoid this problem the triangle must be cleaned. A cloth dipped in thinner (rubber cement thinner, xylene, or lighter fluid) will clean the edge of an acrylic triangle. However, on some triangles, such as those made of polypropylene, the xylene thinners will cause the edges to crack and gum up. If you are having a problem with the thinner, you may try a damp cloth and elbow grease or switch to a metal-edge triangle that is not affected by solvents. Another solution is to cut a number of cardboard strips to use as straightedges and throw them away as you work.

Marker Consistency

You will notice that all markers have a juicy quality when they are new. The way in which the dyes are formulated and the quantity of base they contain will determine how juicy the markers are and, more importantly, how they perform. A juicy marker will tend to bleed excessively and leave blobs of color at the end of each stroke, making it frustrating and difficult to use. Some brands are said to go from juicy to dry without a good working period in between. In others the juicy stage is short and there is a long working life before the marker dries out.

Wool felt is the traditional nib material for markers. Some new brands and most fine points have a synthetic tip of dacron, nylon, or a cast plastic. The flow characteristics of the various tips depend more upon the formulation of the colors than on the nib. Some manufacturers claim a synthetic tip lays color down faster and more evenly than a wool tip. Others say a wool tip is firmer and keeps its shape better in larger nibs. The characteristic of all nibs that is of most concern, other than size, is their tendency to dry out if left uncapped. A dry tip does not mean the marker is out of dye. If the tip can be rejuvenated or changed, the marker will be saved. Wool tips are difficult to rejuvenate and may develop annoying hard spots. Synthetic tips, however, are more easily rejuvenated by dipping them into a solvent for a moment or sometimes by recapping overnight.

Selecting a Palette

Selecting a working palette of markers will depend upon their intended use and the paper you plan to work with.

In addition to a basic palette, having a series of fine-point grays is very helpful when rendering. The fine-point nib markers should be slightly narrower than the narrowest line produced by the standard broad tip. A marker with too fine a line may be good for line drawing and sketching, but it will not produce a line strong enough to hold up visually in a rendering.

The following are sample selections for red palettes in the various marker brands. This is primarily for purposes of example. I advise you to choose your own palettes depending upon rendering needs.

Mecanorma	Prismacolor Art Marker	AD
289 Cherry Pink	PM–9 Apple Blossom	Pumpkin P150
242 Middle Red	PM–6 Scarlet	Sanguine P65
124 Red	PM–5 Scarlet Lake	Saffron P66

187 Crimson	PM–4 Crimson	Vermilion P76
181 Red Wood	PM–2 Chinese Red	Life Red P80
262 Dark Brown		Tobacco P60

Berol Art Markers	**Design**	**Pantone**
8928	336 Red L0	176–M
8921	336 Red L1	211–M
8922	326 Red Orange L2	232–M
8924	336 Red L	219–M
8944	336 Red L8	Rhodamine Red–M
	336 Red L9	Rubine Red–M
	213 Red Brown L8	259–M

As shown by the above examples, you can gather a larger palette in some brands than in others. The color balance also ranges from a very orange red to a cool violet red depending upon the brand. This may be annoying, but not necessarily limiting, as exact color matches are not essential in rendering. The exact product color will be identified by code numbers or color swatches that may accompany the presentation.

Common Marker Brands

AD Markers

Range: 200 permanent colors, including grays and black. AD Markers offer four different interchangeable nibs: a very wide brush nib, the standard wedge, a bullet nib, and a fine point.

Grays: Warm and cool grays from #1 through #10

Base: Xylol

Tip: Wool felt on brush and wedge
Synthetic on bullet and fine point

Related Products: 66 Aquadyes Markers (watercolor broad tip)
66 Aquadyes Watercolor Dyes
24 Water-base fine-point tech markers

AD Markers use a system of interchangeable nibs so that any one of four nibs can be plugged into a marker. The great advantage of this system is for a marker whose nib has dried out, usually from being left uncapped. A new nib can be put in, bringing the marker back to life. It is not practical to continuously switch nibs on any one marker, because the nibs cannot be reused; the marker dries out faster, and it takes time for the dye to saturate the new nib. However, it is very convenient to be able to put specific points on certain markers (e.g., a brush nib on a black or background color), to change nibs occasionally, or to

make a set of fine-point grays. When a new tip is put in it takes only a moment for it to be saturated for use. The wedge nib is slightly larger than that on other marker brands. Many people like this as larger areas may be covered, thus enabling you to work faster.

The AD Marker color range is extensive. It does not conform to a specific color wheel, but does offer a very complete range of primary and secondary colors (yellows, greens, blues, violets, reds, and oranges) as well as grays, browns, and architectural colors.

The three water-base companion products to AD Markers—Aquadyes, Aquadyes Watercolor Dyes, and ultra-fine Tech markers—are useful additions to the line. They may be worked under or over the permanent color without bleeding or smudging. They are particularly useful in backgrounds as they can be worked without affecting the permanent rendering. The liquid dyes allow you to work with an airbrush or a cotton pad.

Design Art Markers (Eberhard Faber)

Range: 120 broad-tip markers, including grays and black
72 fine-point markers
48 ultra fine-point markers

Gray: #2 through #9, cool gray
#4 through #7, warm gray

Base: Xylene type

Tip: Wool felt on broad tips
Synthetic on fine points

Related Products: 60 Colorama colored pencils
60 Nupastel colored chalks

The color range of Design Art Markers is based on a simple color wheel. Each hue (color family) is identified by a code number, followed by the letter 'L' (for example, red is 336-L). The 'L' indicates that this is the full intensity of that color. Tints (light values) of a color are identified by the numbers 0, 1, and 2 following the L, with 0 being the lightest tint. Shades (dark values) of a color are identified by the numbers 8 and 9 following the L, with 9 being the darkest. Therefore a marker labeled 336-L1 indicates a red (336) of a medium light value (L1). Design Markers divide a color wheel into twenty-four parts, offering all of the primary colors (yellow, red and, blue); all of the secondary colors (green, orange, and violet); all of the tertiary colors (yellow green, yellow orange, red orange, red violet, blue violet, and blue green) and some others for a total of eighteen of the twenty-four possible hues.

In addition to this breakdown, Design Markers offer twenty-four "fashion colors" that are popular in fashion design and twelve wood-tone markers. They fill out their color selection with twenty additional hues, tints, and shades. While there is no extensive range in any one designated hue (e.g., red-336 plus two tints and two shades), a good palette can be made up from the marker selection.

Design Markers offer a full range of cool grays based on the eight steps that approximate the visual gray range of television. The darkest, gray-9, is one visual step down from black. Each gray thereafter is half the density of the one before it. Therefore, two layers of gray-8 will equal gray-9. There are four warm grays that are intended to approximate the four grays in newspaper printing. Naturally, these are middle-range grays (4,5,6 and 7) and again are at one-half density steps from each other.

The fine-point markers have flexible plastic tips which can make a good line for detailing and sketching or a broad stroke when used on the side. The ultra fine-point markers produce, as you might expect, a very fine line.

Eberhard Faber also offers Colorama colored pencils and Nupastel chalks, both of which coordinate well with markers for rendering and are of good quality.

Mecanorma Art Markers

Range: 92 broad-tip markers, including grays and black
92 fine-tip markers matching the broad tip markers

Grays: 11 steps of cool gray
11 steps of warm gray

Base: Alcohol type

Nib: Nylon (synthetic)

Related Products: The Mecanorma system includes colored films, colored papers, gradated papers, and other graphic arts products.

This is a relatively new marker with some unique features. It has a very lightweight aluminum barrel. The nib is smaller than the traditional wedge and is beveled to a chiseled edge rather than a flat surface. This nib shape is convenient for rendering as it is easier to see and control the ends of your strokes. In addition, the tip of the marker makes a nice "bullet nib" line.

The nylon tip delivers the color very rapidly. This allows for a juicy quality throughout the life of the marker and enables you to get an instant color density with light pressure. The density remains constant for the entire length of a stroke.

By exerting less pressure on the nib, its life will be extended as it will not get soft and mushy. One nice feature of the synthetic nib is that if the marker is left uncapped and the tip dries out, recapping it for forty-eight hours will rejuvenate it, provided the marker is not out of ink. The nylon nib may also be cut and reshaped with a sharp blade or sandpaper block.

Mecanorma's color range centers on the most commonly used colors: reds, greens, blues, browns, and grays, each with a good selection of tints and shades. The color range has a particularly strong set of pastels. The fine-point markers match the broad tips in color and are excellent for detailing and sketching. The fine point is protected by a plastic collar to prevent breakdown by too much pressure or rubbing against a sharp-edge rule.

Mecanorma's companion graphic products are coordinated with their markers, making it convenient to switch from rendering to layout work.

Pantone Markers (Letraset)

Range: 203 broad-tip markers, including grays and black
105 fine-tip markers

Grays: 11 warm grays, from #1 through #11
11 cool grays, from #1 through #11

Base: Xylene type on broad-tip markers
Alcohol on fine-tip markers

Tip: Wool felt, broad tip
Synthetic, fine tip

Related Products: Color-coordinated graphic arts products. Pantone Markers, as the name implies, are color coordinated to the Pantone Color System.

Letraset offers a wide selection of markers, papers, inks, films, and other products, all color-coordinated and coded to each other. This system is intended for the design of printed material and is not really important for rendering. The color range of Pantone Markers is very extensive. They offer a wide selection of hues from around the color wheel. These, along with the color-coordinated products, are very helpful to graphic designers. These hues are complemented with a good offering of "toned down" or pastel markers that are intended for product and architectural rendering.

The fine-point markers match the colors of the most popular broad-tip markers. However, the fine-point grays are incomplete with only two or three markers each in the warm and cool ranges.

Two companion products of the markers are Letraset heavy marker paper (M3) and the Letrajet. The marker paper is a good-quality marker paper that is slightly more absorbent than most others. It gives deeper colors, yet there is very little bleeding. The Letrajet is a unique little device that attaches to a fine-point marker and permits designers to achieve an airbrush effect. Basically, it blows a stream of air that picks up color from the marker and "airbrushes" it onto the paper. Because this tool relies on the juicyness and flow of a marker, large areas cannot be covered uniformly. However, for small areas and special effects, the Letrajet is convenient and fun.

Prismacolor Art Markers

Berol USA makes an unusual series of double-ended markers with a fine-point nib at one end and a broad nib at the other. This makes the markers very convenient to use and economical, since one set contains both fine- and broad-tip markers.

Range: 116 markers, including grays and black
Grays: Both warm and cool, from #1 through #9
Base: Alcohol
Related products: 60 Prismacolor Art Pencils
             48 Verithin Prismacolor Art Pencils
             48 Prismacolor Art Stix

The color range of these markers offers a good selection from all of the basic hues. The markers are arranged numerically by color groups: PM1–PM12, reds; PM13–PM24, oranges and yellows; PM25–PM36, greens; PM37–PM48, blues; PM49–PM60, magentas and violets. The remainder of the markers (PM61–PM116) are divided into architectural colors, wood colors, warm grays, and cool grays. This system makes it very easy to select a palette for rendering, as the initial grouping has already been done.

The Prismacolor Art Pencils, Verithin Pencils, and Art Stix are excellent media for detailing and finishing a rendering. The pencils come in sixty of the most popular drawing colors, including metallics. The Art Stix are essentially the same as the pencils, but are slightly softer.

Berol Art Markers

Range: 46 broad-tip colored markers, including grays and black
             1 fine-point black marker
Grays: 5 warm grays at 10%, 20%, 40%, 60%, and 80%
             5 cool grays at 10%, 20%, 40%, 60%, and 80%

Base: Alcohol
Tip: Bonded nylon
Related products: Prismacolor Art Pencils
             Prismacolor Art Stix

Despite the limited palette of forty-six markers, there is a very useful selection for color sketching with at least four markers in each of the four major colors (yellow, green, blue, and red orange) as well as grays and accent colors.

Sources of Supply

The following is a list of companies that offer art markers for designers:

Design Art Markers
Eberhard Faber, Inc.
Crestwood
Wilkes-Barre, PA 18703

Prismacolor Art Markers
Berol USA
Danbury, CT 06810

AD Markers
Chartpak
One River Road
Leeds, MA 01053

Pantone Color Markers
Letraset USA
40 Eisenhower Drive
Paramus, NJ 07652

Mecanorma Art Markers
Normacolor
Martin Instrument Company
13450 Farmington Road
Livonia, MI 48150

Appendix B
Rendering Checklist

The following checklist may be helpful in planning a rendering. The bulk of the checklist deals with the communication of the concept and of the use of the product. Both of these concerns can be translated into visual clues in the rendering for a more effective presentation. It is important that a rendering have a focus or serve a specific purpose. You will then try to describe these important aspects of a design in the simplest manner. The checklist will help you think through the product so that it can be sufficiently detailed in the rendering. It will also suggest elements for the background and page composition to further support the design concept.

Many of the considerations listed may be obvious in some products. For example, a digital readout indicates both the technology (p.c. boards and microchips) and the fact that the product is electronic. Switches may indicate scale since they are made to fit the finger. Of course not everything about a product can be indicated in one rendering, so consider the most important elements of your concept and plan your rendering around them.

Checklist: Basic Rendering

I. Form: visualizing a product as existing in three-dimensional space requires a clear, accurate description of the form.
   A. Describe the basic volume in perspective.
   B. Show changes in levels and positions of major elements.
   C. Establish a clear value system (1,2,3) and good contrast.
   D. Add highlights where appropriate.
   E. Use shadows to help "pop" details.
II. Materials and Details: the surface quality of an object is described by the action of light on the materials and the delineation of minor details such as parting lines, switches, and readouts.
   A. Consider the reflections onto the product from both specific parts and details and generalized reflections from the background and the environment.
   B. Transparent areas should show the distortion of lines, collection of values in the edges, and glare.
   C. Texture on surfaces should be suggested, particularly at the focal point.
   D. Add highlights, shade, and shadows in parting lines and details.

III. Scale and Object Identity: indicate what the product is and the size relationship to the user.
   A. Put familiar objects into the rendering. This may include a part on the product itself.
   B. Show some human interaction with the product such as a hand holding it or a figure standing by it.
   C. Put some simple dimensions on the product or as part of the background.
IV. Use and Use Situation: show the product in such a way that we understand how it is to be used. Show its primary function and where it will be used, if this is not evident from the design of the product.
   A. Show the product in its working position rather than closed for storage or from an odd angle.
   B. Have other elements that may be needed for its operation indicated, or show someone using the product.
   C. Include simple auxiliary drawings of its use.
V. Environment: describe the setting in which the product will typically be used so that it can be better understood in terms of materials, storage, and support elements.
   A. Try to use the environment as a background.
   B. Use short verbal statements as necessary.
   C. Use auxiliary drawings as necessary.
VI. Mechanics: indicate the systems that are needed to operate the product and perhaps the basic technology of the product.
   A. Be attentive to small clues (plugs and the like).
   B. Suggest support systems in the background.
   C. Accompany the rendering with auxiliary technical drawings.
VII. Details: include any other special information, features, or extras that are important to the concept. For example, a modular furniture system may need line drawings of various configurations to show its versatility.
   A. Add plane view drawings to one side of the rendering.
   B. Refer to other drawings.
   C. Use written information or title blocks.

Bibliography

D'Amelio, Joseph. *Perspective Drawing Handbook*. New York: Van Nostrand Reinhold Company, 1984.
> Explains and illustrates the concepts of perspective and the choices and techniques available to the designer in laying out drawings.

Doblin, Jay. *Perspective: A New System for Designers*. New York: Watson Guptill Publications, 1956.
> Presents a very good system for quickly setting up and drawing in perspective. Allows for combination of mechanical and freehand drawing.

Doyle, Michael. *Color Drawing*. New York: Van Nostrand Reinhold Company, 1981.
> A very good manual for architectural rendering with markers and colored pencils.

Gill, Robert. *The VNR Manual of Rendering with Pen and Ink, rev. ed.* New York: Van Nostrand Reinhold Company, 1984.
> Provides techniques of using Rapidographs and ink pens for architectural black-and-white rendering.

Hanks, Kurt, and Belliston, Larry. *Draw!: A Visual Approach to Thinking, Learning, and Communicating*. Los Altos: William Kauffman, Inc., 1977.
> This book helps develop skills in idea sketching and using thumbnails as effective thinking tools.

Hanks, Kurt, and Belliston, Larry. *Rapid Viz: A New Method for Rapid Visualization of Ideas*. Los Altos: William Kauffman, Inc., 1980.
> This is a how-to formula for sketching your ideas. It does not go into presentation sketches or marker techniques.

Leach, Sid. *Techniques of Interior Design Rendering and Presentation*. New York: McGraw Hill, Inc., 1978.
> A very good how-to manual for interior rendering and making presentations.

Martin, C. Leslie. *Design Graphics*, 2nd ed. New York: Macmillan Inc., 1968.
> Technical drafting manual for orthographics, paraline drawing, perspective, shadows, and some rendering. Easy to understand and thorough.

Maxwell, David. *Rendering with Design Markers*. Eberhard Faber, Inc. Series of four booklets on rendering stone, plastic, metal, and wood. They are basic, but the information is sound.

Munsell, A.H. *A Color Notation*. Baltimore: Munsell Color Company, Inc.
> Comes with student color charts and a color wheel. Explains the Munsell color system very clearly.

Ramsey, C.G., and Sleeper, H.R., eds. *Architectural Graphic Standards, 7th ed.* New York: John Wiley & Sons, Inc., 1981.

Welling, Richard. *Drawing with Markers*. New York: Watson Guptill Publications, 1974.
> A manual for using markers in a free-sketch style. Includes landscapes, still lifes, etc.

Index